Sin, Sheep and Scotsmen

John George Adair and the Derryveagh evictions, 1861

Sin, Sheep and Scotsmen

John George Adair and the Derryveagh evictions, 1861

W. E. Vaughan

Appletree Press
and
The Ulster Society
for Irish Historical Studies

First published and printed in 1983 by
The Appletree Press Ltd
7 James Street South
Belfast BT2 8DL
in association with
The Ulster Society
for Irish Historical Studies

Copyright © W. E. Vaughan, 1983

Cover photograph: Co. Fermanagh
eviction scene, c. 1880 (Lawrence collection,
National Library of Ireland).

British Library Cataloguing in Publication Data

Vaughan, W. E.
  Sin, Sheep and Scotsmen.—(Explorations in
Irish history, ISSN 0263-2799; 2)
  1. Eviction—Derryveagh (Ireland)—
History—19th century
  I. Title   II. Series
  33.5'4   HD1511.I73

ISBN 0-86281-108-2

for M.

Acknowledgements

I wish to acknowledge the generous financial assistance given towards the publication of this book by the Grace Lawless Lee Fund, Trinity College, Dublin, and by the Ulster Society for Irish Historical Studies. I wish to thank the custodians of those record repositories mentioned in the references at pp 69–75 for permission to refer to documents in their possession. I also wish to thank Dr T. W. Moody for reading a draft of this work; Dr Brian Walker for asking me to contribute to Explorations in Irish History; John Cornforth for giving me information about Adair's career in the U.S.A.; and Rory Bland of Rath House, Ballybrittas, for showing me the graves of Adair and Edward Shepherd Mead.

20 December 1982
W. E. Vaughan
26 Trinity College
Dublin 2

Contents

List of Illustrations

Adair's estate in County Donegal, 1861

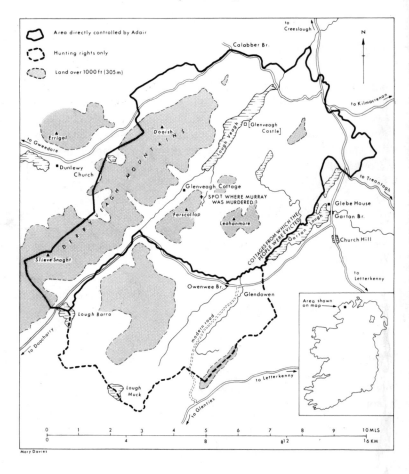

Area directly controlled by Adair

Hunting rights only

Land over 1000 ft (305 m)

to Creeslough

N

Calabber Br.

to Kilmacrenan

Errigal

Dooish S

Lough Veagh

□[Glenveagh Castle]

to Gweedore

Dunlewy Church

D E R R Y V E A G H   M O U N T A I N S

Glenveagh Cottage

+ SPOT WHERE MURRAY WAS MURDERED

to Treantagh

Glebe House
Gartan Br.

Farscollop

Leahanmore

Gartan Lough

Church Hill

COTTAGES FROM WHICH THE PEOPLE WERE EVICTED

to Letterkenny

Slieve Snaght

Owenwee Br.

Glendowen

Lough Barra

modern road

to Doocharry

Area shown on map

Lough Muck

to Letterkenny

to Glenties

0   1   2   3   4   5   6   7   8   9   10 MLS

0   4   8   12   16 KM

Mary Davies

1 The evictions

The sixteen townlands of the district of Derryveagh lie to the north and west of the small village of Church Hill on the road west from Letterkenny. On the morning of Monday, 8 April 1861, the sub-sheriff of the County Donegal, Samuel Crookshank, accompanied by a special force of 200 constables, proceeded along the rough, unfinished road that stretched along the north-western shore of Lough Gartan to Lough Barra in the west, evicting from their houses and lands the 47 families who lived in Derryveagh. By 10 April the work was finished: 244 persons, comprising 85 adults and 159 children, were evicted; 28 houses unroofed or levelled; 11,602 acres of virtually barren land cleared of human habitation. The desolation was only slightly mitigated by the restoration of about a fifth of those evicted as caretakers of their former holdings.[1]

Frequently and erroneously referred to as the Glenveagh evictions, from the name of the castle later built by the owner of the estate, John George Adair of Bellegrove in the Queen's County, the Derryveagh evictions aroused a great amount of public interest: they were debated in parliament;[2] the correspondence between Adair and the Irish government was published as a parliamentary paper;[3] every aspect of Adair's estate management was investigated not only by the government and the police but by the newspapers as well. According to the *Freeman's Journal*, for example, the evictions were 'the largest, and attended with the most painful circumstances, that have occurred in Donegal, or indeed in any other part of Ireland'. The *Londonderry Standard* attempted to convey the horror of the proceedings by noting that 'the police officers themselves could not refrain from weeping' and that the sub-sheriff was so moved by the plight of one old man that he offered to pay for his conveyance to the workhouse in Letterkenny. *The Nation* hinted darkly that 'bad work has been done in Donegal; work full of sorrow and of sin; work that will bear bitter and bloody fruit'.[4]

As well as widespread publicity in press and parliament, the evictions were the subject of at least two ballads and a novel—the remarkable *Glenveigh, or the victims of vengeance* by Patrick Sarsfield Cassidy, published less than ten years after the evictions.[5] The only element of publicity missing was one of those engravings in the *Illustrated London News* that were so typical of a later phase of landlord-tenant conflict in Ireland: the evictions were mentioned in that weekly, but not illustrated, competing unsuccessfully with Cossacks attacking a religious procession in Warsaw, an omnibus plunging into the canal at Portobello bridge in Dublin, Lord Ranelagh at a military review in Brighton, and Madingley Hall, seat of the Prince of Wales, then an undergraduate at Cambridge.[6]

Although much of the reporting in the newspapers was highly coloured, its fundamental authenticity can be established by the confidential report of the poor-law inspector, Robert Hamilton, who had seen nothing like the Derryveagh evictions 'since the evictions in Mayo in 1847'.[7] The official terseness of his report is as moving in its own way as anything published in the newspapers: old Owen Ward of Drumnalifferney, after repeated warnings to quit his holding, kissed the walls of his house 'and each member of his family did the same and then left'. The simple enumeration of each family evicted—its circumstances and fate—is made more shocking than anything in *Glenveigh, or the victims of vengeance* by the sudden occurrence, in what is simply a prosaic list, of statements such as: 'this family seem to be wandering through the ruins of the houses'. (A. M. Sullivan was probably exaggerating only slightly when he claimed that sub-sheriffs found evictions 'more painful to their feelings' than even 'the odious and distressing... duties they had to perform at an execution on the public scaffold'.[8])

The memory of the evictions did not diminish after 1861: they were almost certainly the original of the evictions in Allingham's *Laurence Bloomfield in Ireland*;[9] Cassidy's novel was published in 1870; Father Lavelle mentioned them in his great indictment of Irish landlordism, *The Irish landlord since the revolution*, characteristically exaggerating the number of those evicted;[10] A. M. Sullivan devoted a whole chapter to them in *New Ireland*; tourist guides of the late nineteenth century referred to 'Mr Adair of eviction notoriety' long after he was dead;[11] Stephen Gwynn devoted three pages and much speculation to them in

John George Adair 1823–85

his *Highways and byways in Donegal and Antrim*.[12] In more recent times, Dominic Ó Ceallaigh, the Donegal historian, composed a commemorative ode of twenty-one stanzas for their centenary in 1961.[13] In 1979 Professor Alistair Rowan referred to them in his admirable *North west Ulster*, writing that Adair 'disappeared one night on the lough, never to be seen again', a nice piece of providential symmetry not in fact realized, since Adair died in a hotel in St Louis, Missouri, in 1885.[14] In 1980 Liam Dolan published his *Land war and eviction in Derryveagh 1840–65*, concentrating largely on the material in the Larcom papers and the registered papers of the Chief Secretary's Office.[15] Finally, in 1982 two articles in *Country Life* by John Cornforth set Glenveagh Castle firmly in its historical context by describing the evictions.[16]

2 Background

The background to the evictions was, on the surface at least, simple enough. The Derryveagh estate had been acquired by Adair in December 1859;[17] a quarrel between Adair and his tenants about shooting rights and trespassing sheep culminated in the murder of his Scottish steward, James Murray, in November 1860; the police having failed to detect Murray's murderers, he determined to evict all of the Derryveagh tenants whom he believed to be implicated in the murder; in April 1861, therefore, 47 families were evicted by the sub-sheriff, the notices to quit, served ten months *before* Murray's death, having conveniently expired in November 1860.

Derryveagh was not Adair's only acquisition in County Donegal. Since 1857 he had also acquired the neighbouring Glenveagh and Gartan estates, making with Derryveagh an area of about 28,000 acres. (He had also acquired hunting rights over a large area near his actual estates, thus giving some substance to his grandiloquent claim in the 1870s to the ownership of an estate of 42,000 acres in County Donegal.)[18] According to his own account, he had acquired this vast estate, most of which was either worthless or worth at most only a few pence an acre, because he had been 'enchanted by the surpassing beauty of the scenery'. His strongest wish was 'to open up these remote districts and to elevate and improve the condition of the people'. It is possible that his purchases of land in Donegal were prompted by an altruistic romanticism: the ornately battlemented house he later built at Glenveagh suggests that he had his share of the contemporary taste for Gothic revivalism; his confusing renaming of his family seat, Bellegrove, as 'Rathdaire' suggests a liking for the pretentious side of landownership;[19] the extensive re-building at Bellegrove in the 1860s and 1870s, both in its style and scale, also suggests a desire to impress visitors with the seigneurial grandeur of the family.[20] Neither altruism nor romantic pretentiousness are incompatible with a good eye for the main chance; but while the former qualities in Adair can only be inferred from his surroundings, there is no doubt that he was a vigorous and successful speculator in land, the purchase of a barren waste in a remote county notwithstanding.

Between 1852 and his first purchase of land in Donegal in 1857, he had spent almost £35,000 on the purchase of land in different parts of Ireland: he bought land in Tipperary in 1852 (two lots), in 1853, 1855, and 1856 (three lots); in Kilkenny in 1853; and in the Queen's County in 1857. In all he bought nine lots comprising over 4,800 acres.[21] (It is difficult to translate nineteenth-century money into modern values but a multiple of 100 does not seem inappropriate: beef cost 6d a pound and an agricultural labourer's wages rarely exceeded 1s. 6d. a day in the 1860s.) But between 1857 and 1861 his energies were concentrated on Donegal: he bought no land elsewhere in that period; after the evictions in April 1861, he returned to the pursuit of landed wealth outside Donegal.

At first sight Adair was an unlikely land speculator; he was not the typical, hard-faced merchant who had done well during the great famine—the typical land shark of contemporary demonology—but the only son and heir of a small but well established landed family in the Queen's County. His grandfather was not a 'ploughman poor' as the ballad, 'The lovers of Glenveagh', claimed: his paternal grandfather was a gentleman whose family had been settled in the Queen's County since the seventeenth century and his maternal grandfather was the dean of Kildare. His father, George, was a noted agricultural improver: a model of his farm buildings at Bellegrove was erected on Leinster Lawn during the Great Exhibition in Dublin in 1853 and later presented to the R.D.S.; he was a partner of William Dargan in a pioneering venture manufacturing sugar from sugar-beet in Mount-mellick; his massive farming operations at Bellegrove gave 'a vast amount of well and promptly paid employment' to local people.[22] ('Would that we had many more resident, non-absentee, stay-at-home proprietors, such as Mr Adair amongst us' was the concluding sentence of an article in the *Irish Farmers' Gazette* about George Adair and 'his active and energetic son', published in 1855.) Nor was John George the coarse, ignorant lout depicted by Cassidy in *Glenveigh, or the victims of vengeance*—'a man who got a little education in a charity school in one of the highland shires of Scotland'[23]—but well enough educated by the standards of his day. After a private education he entered Trinity College, Dublin, in 1839, at the age of sixteen, and graduated in 1843. Attendance at Trinity, while it gave him a passable prose style and a flexible attitude towards accuracy, placed him in the second rank of Irish landed society: below the peerage and the largest landed proprietors and firmly in that class of small, resident gentry who often combined estate management with large-scale farming, and the summit of whose local greatness was a deputy-lieutenantship.

The importance of popular aspersions on Adair's background and education lay not in their abusiveness but in the apparent reluctance of contemporaries to believe that the perpetrator of such a terrible deed as the Derryveagh evictions was a member of the old gentry and a man of substance. His restless ambition, apparent greed and considerable business acumen were not, however, unconnected with his family background. His father may have been an energetic, stay-at-home farmer, content with his paternal acres; but through his mother, Adair was related to one of the most remarkable landed families in nineteenth-century Ireland: she was a niece of the first Lord Ashtown, one of the largest landlords in the country and, more importantly, one of her brothers was William Steuart Trench, author of the inaccurately named *Realities of Irish Life* and one of the most controversial land agents of his generation. It is possible that Adair, whose mother died just after his birth, spent much of his childhood with his Trench cousins, especially the brilliant and erratic, John Townsend Trench, William Steuart's second son and inventor of, among other things, 'Trench's Tubeless Tyre' and a commercially successful 'cure' for epilepsy consisting only of coloured water.[24] There is evidence of close contacts between the two men in later years: John Townsend was almost certainly the designer of Glenveagh Castle, and in 1874 he married the daughter of a neighbour of Adair's in County Donegal—

Leonora, daughter of George Cecil Gore Wray of Ardnamona.[25]

The Trenchs, who were in some ways to the nineteenth century what the Beresfords had been to the eighteenth—numerous, ubiquitous, and well-connected—were often insensitive and aggressive in their dealings with the tenants on the estates they managed. One of their critics, commenting on William Steuart's management of the enormous Digby estate in the barony of Geashill in the King's County, stated:

> When leases are to be broken, when independent rights are to be extinguished, or 'contracted away', when an overcrowded estate is to be thinned at the least possible cost to the owner, when a rebellious tenantry are to be subdued, and Ribbonmen are to be banished or hanged, Mr Trench is the man to do the work of improvement.[26]

As agents of the Bath, Lansdowne, and Digby estates their experience of tenants was wide and varied; in addition, William Steuart took a practical and successful interest in farming, winning prizes for some of his experiments; but above all their tempers were uncertain: William Steuart enjoying face-to-face clashes with recalcitrant tenants, and John Townsend indulging a waggish and truculent sense of humour— he plunged the Lansdowne estate in the Queen's County into disorder during the land war by poking heavy fun at the fat leader of a deputation of tenants.[27] They brought an unhealthy insistence on the rights of property and the virtues of innovation to a business that was best conducted on more conservative principles.

In 1868 William Steuart Trench published his remarkable apologia, *Realities of Irish Life*, a highly coloured account of his own and his family's experience of managing Irish estates.[28] As unwitting testimony to the ineptly patronising manner he adopted in his dealings with his social inferiors, the book is most revealing; as an essay in historical truth it hardly lives up to its title; there was no mention, for example, of his nephew's activities in County Donegal. The illustrations in the first edition show the Trenchs as they saw themselves—smooth-browed, officiously moustached, their eyes firmly fixed on the horizon, seeing life steadily even if they did not see it whole. It may have been something of their lynx-eyed myopia that plunged their kinsman, Adair, into quarrels with his tenants in Donegal; equally, it may have been his connection with a large landed family that engendered his ambition to turn land speculator, rather than to follow his father as a stay-at-home improver. While it is impossible to prove that Adair was directly advised by the Trenchs during the troubles on his Donegal estate between 1857 and 1861, the quarrel that he initiated there, culminating in the murder of his steward in 1860 and the evictions in 1861, could, with a certain amount of rewriting, form a chapter of *Realities*.

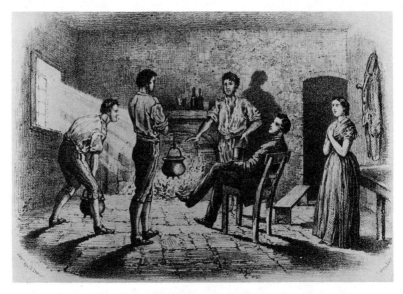

William Steuart Trench on a domiciliary visit. The caption of the original was: 'Who are these men', said I, 'and what are they doing here!' 'We were distilling poteen', said one of them, 'would your honor like to taste some!'

What is clear, however, is that Adair and his uncle, William Steuart Trench, were almost certainly in touch with each other in these years: in 1858, for example, they attended meetings of the Royal Agricultural Improvement Society of Ireland in Dublin.[29] What is also clear, is that the Trenchs were involved in a dispute, similar in important respects to Adair's, with the tenants on Lord Digby's estate in the barony of Geashill near Tullamore in 1859–62, coinciding with Adair's troubles in Donegal. In some respects the two disputes were different: the Trenchs did not evict large numbers of tenants at Geashill, but leases had been broken and some squatters removed. Also, no one was murdered at Geashill, although Thomas Weldon Trench, Adair's cousin, was informed in February 1860 that 'Darby Flanagan of Pigeonhouse has £20 collected for the shooting of you'.[30] Similarities between the two disputes were, however, striking. First, Adair and the Trenchs believed that they were the victims of arson attempts, although there was evidence that in both cases the fires had started accidentally: a fire in the outhouses of the rectory at Church Hill, where Adair was staying after the murder of Murray, was claimed by him to be arson, but seems to have been an accident; in March 1860, an apparent attempt to burn down Geashill Castle was made, but later it appeared that the fire was caused by Trench's own servants.[31] Secondly, Adair and the Trenchs quarrelled with the police in their localities: in December 1859, for example, William Steuart Trench complained to Sir Thomas Larcom that 'such slothfulness, such utter uselessness as I have seen in the police in the barony of Geashill in the King's County I have never seen in my life'.[32] (In quarrelling with the police, the Trenchs went further and fared worse than Adair: he successfully abandoned the police to face litigation that he had caused, but the Trenchs had to pay over £200 in costs and damages to a police-man whom they claimed had been found drunk in a ditch.[33]) Thirdly, both were convinced that they were the victims of a widespread and powerful conspiracy of Ribbonmen among their tenants. In March 1860, Trench claimed, in terms that would have been endorsed by his nephew, that his son, Thomas Weldon, was 'hunted ...by numbers of Ribbonmen, with the skill, the ferocity, and apparently with all the pleasurable excitement of a Gordon Cumming* in chase after a tiger or hyena'.[34] It is likely, therefore, that events in the King's County and Donegal were connected by the shared ideas of Adair and the Trenchs: dimly understood events in the one were transformed by half truths generated in the other, and discrete events were arranged and connected in patterns whose inspiration was shared ideas about the incompetence of the police and the pervasiveness of Ribbonism.

At first Adair's actions in Donegal were high-handed rather than harsh: he erected a pound for stray goats and sheep found trespassing on his land; he quarrelled about shooting rights with a neighbouring

---

* Roualeyn George Gordon-Cumming (1820–66) was an African lion hunter who went about the country lecturing and exhibiting his lion skins; according to the *D.N.B.*, 'he obtained great popularity, and made a good deal of money'.

landlord, becoming involved in a brawl that led to his prosecution for assault; he evicted two tenants, giving them compensation, but less than they claimed as the value of their farms; in July 1859 he ordered the arrest of four of the Derryveagh tenants whom he accused of stealing his sheep. (This was five months before he actually became landlord of the Derryveagh estate.) They were later released for lack of evidence against them and complained to the lord lieutenant—supported by a local magistrate, Lt-Col. Humfrey—of their harsh and illegal treatment, being arrested 'without *any warrant* from a magistrate, or other legal authority, but by the *verbal directions* of *Mr Adair alone*... being marched through the country as felons, for a distance, backwards and forwards, of upwards of sixty miles'. This incident, which culminated in the arrested peasants prosecuting the police for illegal arrest, brought Adair into disfavour with the police whom he left in the lurch by denying that he had given authority for the arrests.

As simple incidents of estate management, these disputes might in time have been forgotten; what made them potentially serious was their connection with Adair's taking up sheep-farming on a large scale. The introduction of imported Scots sheep, accompanied by Scots shepherds, had caused an outbreak of serious disorder on Lord George Hill's estate at Gweedore several years before: the tenants killed hundreds of sheep because they feared eviction; several tenants were convicted of maliciously killing the sheep and one was transported and several imprisoned.[35] When landlords introduced large-scale sheep-farming, tenants were deprived of mountain pastures that they had long used freely; also, they felt threatened with eviction from the patches of fertile land they held in the valleys. In the absence of fences, the new sheep-farmers expected the tenants to keep their stock from wandering on the reserved pastures: apart from loss of grass, trespassing sheep included ill-bred rams which consorted with the well-bred Scots ewes, with results deplored by the shepherds. It was to protect what he regarded as his own pastures that Adair erected a pound in May 1858; it was observed in May 1861, for example, that 40 cows and horses, taken by Adair's shepherds from the mountains, were at one time in the pound at Glenveagh; to have these released 'the owners had to pay 1s. 6d. for each horse, and 1s. 3d. for each cow'.

The problems of sheep-farming were exacerbated by the character of the shepherds, mainly Scotsmen, some of whom combined strict ideas about the rights of property with loose notions of how to protect them. Of the group of Scotsmen who came within the knowledge of the police during the events in Derryveagh, the best that can be said of their moral character was that their faults had the doubtful merit of simplicity: perjury, theft, murder, adultery were at one time or another imputed to them. Two of them, Dugald Rankin and Adam Grierson, spent time in prison between 1861 and 1863; two of them, James Murray and Adam Grierson, were murdered; and two of them were suspected of murder by the police. The loss of sheep by malicious killing on Lord George Hill's estate had given the shepherds the idea of fraudulently claiming compensation for malicious damage, levied as a rate on the locality where the crime occurred, for sheep that had died naturally of exposure—the only original idea contributed to the business of sheep-farming by these shepherds. In February 1860, for example, Adair's shepherds claimed compensation for the malicious destruction of 85 'Scotch' sheep, but after a thorough search by the police, 65 were found dead 'from *exposure, want* and *neglect* on the part of the shepherds'; also, 16 hides were found in the house of James Murray, the steward. (Murray was able to combine this sort of rascality with officiously helping the police to pursue poteen-makers who were on an island in Lough Veagh, an incident that had made him even more unpopular with local people.)

By November 1860 the tension between Adair and his tenants came to a head when notices to quit, served in January 1860 on the Derryveagh tenants, expired amidst rumours that he was negotiating with English and Scottish sheep-farmers. Adair later claimed that the notices had been served with 'the unanimous wish of the tenants' in order 'to survey and rearrange, in the most equitable and convenient way, the various holdings'. The tenants, he claimed, knew his intentions and 'all gave up possession, with one or two exceptions'. What Adair's real intentions were at this point is not clear: he may or may not have intended to take over a part of the mountain pasture enjoyed by the Derryveagh tenants. What is clear, however, is that the tenants did give peaceable possession, as he claimed, and that no attempt was made at that time to remove them—police reports show that they were left *in situ* after the formal 'eviction' in November.

On the morning of 13 November, almost a fortnight after the expiry of the notices to quit, James Murray left his cottage to look after some sheep in the mountains. He did not return that evening. Two days later a search party found his body on the mountains at the head of Glenveagh: his skull had been fractured with a blow from a large stone; his revolver had been fired once. A coroner's inquest, held a few days later, returned a verdict of murder.

3 Derryveagh and the land question

When, in spite of an energetic search by the police and magistrates, the murderers of Murray were not detected and Adair decided to enforce the notices to quit that had expired, a familiar pattern of landlord–tenant relations seemed to establish itself: friction leading to a murderous conspiracy among the tenants; the landlord defending himself by evicting his tenants. It was, too, a pattern that seemed to be well established in north–west Donegal, with the attempted murder of Rev. Alexander Nixon in October 1858, the destruction of sheep in Gweedore from 1857 on, and the perennial squabbling on the estates of the cantankerous third earl of Leitrim.[36]

The crimes imputed to the tenants provoked in some newspapers a fury equal to that provoked in others by the evictions themselves. After the shooting of Rev. Alexander Nixon, for example, *The Evening Packet* suggested that 'this bloodthirsty tribe of savages be sent off to America ... there will be nothing for it but to clear the land of its wicked population, and plant Christians in their stead'. When James Murray was murdered, the *Express* hoped that 'some means might be devised for making the people suffer for the crime of harbouring murderers. In bad cases this might be eviction. At all events something extraordinary should be done without further delay.' After the evictions took place, the *Northern Whig*, normally sympathetic to the tenants' cause, condemned the conspiracy that had caused them:

> We have often had occasion to denounce Orange outrages, and the narrow and fanatical passions from which they spring. But those outbursts of factious rage do at least take place openly and in the daylight, and are not to be compared in atrocity with the conspiracies to murder and shelter murder, which men know as Ribbonism.[37]

The events in Derryveagh were important not only as a terrible demonstration of the extremes of bitterness reached on one estate, but also as a microcosm of the land question in the whole of Ireland; for coming as they did so soon after the less numerous but equally dramatic evictions at Partry in County Mayo, they could be fitted into what appeared a general trend.[38] (It is worth noting that the Party evictions were debated in parliament after the Derryveagh evictions, although they occurred before them, suggesting the cumulation of interest in them.[39])

Adair seemed to represent a class of landowners frequently criticized in the 1850s and 1860s: purchasers of estates from the Incumbered Estates Commissioners whose task had been to facilitate the sale of heavily mortgaged estates and their transfer to new owners with enough capital to run them successfully. The effect of massive sales in the early 1850s was to attract, not the careful, thriving English capitalists, imbued with English ideas of estate management, but land speculators, often of native origin, whose aim was to make a quick profit. The poverty of the Derryveagh tenants seemed the more extreme when compared with the wealth of their landlord: even at a time of relative agricultural prosperity, the small tenants of Derryveagh—the richest of whom would have been little better off than English agricultural labourers—seemed typical of Irish tenants as a whole, miserable tillers of the soil whose existence was at the mercy of their landlords. The fact that the Derryveagh tenants were evicted without being allowed to sell the tenant-right of their farms not only accentuated their poverty, but breached a custom that was generally believed to maintain better landlord–tenant relations in Ulster than in the other provinces. (One of the advantages of the tenant-right custom was that it gave even evicted tenants a sum of money when quitting their holdings.) Also, the driving out of the native Gaelic speaking population from their ancestral land, where they had dwelt 'for twice a thousand years', and their replacement by Scots sheep touched a common theme of the 1850s and 1860s—the extinction of the Irish race by enforced emigration.[40]

All of these aspects of the Derryveagh evictions—the contrast between rich landlords and poor tenants, the confiscation of tenant-right and improvements, the evil consequences of land speculation, the decline of the Gael and depopulation—were important, but not as important as the two most obvious and dramatic aspects of the affair: first, the apparent violence of relations between landlords and tenants and the inability of the police to detect the perpetrators of agrarian crimes; secondly, the insecurity of tenure suffered by tenants who could be so quickly and easily evicted.

Tenants could be evicted if they owed one year's arrears of rent, or if they remained in their holdings after the expiry of six months' notice to quit. Notices to quit were cheap and easily served; if tenants did not give up possession at the end of the six months, the procedures of the courts, leading to the eventual forcible eviction of the tenants by the sub-sheriff, were not only swift but virtually ineluctable. Adair, for example, served his notices to quit in January 1860; they expired in November 1860; in February 1861, having decided to evict the tenants because they were concealing Murray's murderers, he served them with processes—summonses to attend court to defend their titles; by the beginning of April, only five months after the expiry of the notices to quit, he had a decree from the courts ordering the sheriff to put him in possession of his lands in Derryveagh—a nice verbal inversion of what would actually happen in practice. Having got a decree, practically nothing could stop a landlord from evicting his tenants, if he were determined to do so: the courts had no discretion if the proper forms had been followed; the executive government had no power to halt a civil action and were bound to provide any force required for the protection of the sub-sheriff; the Crown could pardon a murderer, but could not prevent an eviction. Only the full legislative panoply of the state—an act of parliament—could have saved the Derryveagh tenants by April 1861. The only sanction that government could apply to Adair was to remove him from the commission of the peace in County Donegal: a nasty insult to a landed gentleman with territorial ambitions, used, for example, in 1863 to punish Lord Leitrim for insulting the lord lieutenant. Every aspect of Adair's conduct of the evictions was scrutinised by officials, hoping to find a technical irregularity, such as failure to inform the poor-law authorities of his intention to evict families who might need relief;[41] none was found and he was not removed from the commission, the lord chancellor informing Sir Thomas Larcom that such a removal would be 'too strong a measure …merely on the ground of his exercising the rights of property… in the absence of any evidence of *special personal cruelty, or other misconduct*'. Adair was able, therefore, to inflict as heavy a punishment—confiscation of property in the form of tenant-right, and banishment—on the supposed accomplices of his steward's murderers, as the criminal courts would have imposed on them.

The plight of the tenants was one side of the argument. Those who supported the landlord cause fixed their attention on the alleged cause of the evictions: the violence of the peasantry and the inability of the police to detect the perpetrators of agrarian outrages. (Agrarian crime was defined by the police as that part of all crime caused by disputes about the tenure of land.) The record of agrarian crime in Ireland, and in County Donegal in particular, was impressive if taken in isolation. In all Ireland between 1857 and 1878 there were over 100 agrarian homicides, including the murder of Lord Leitrim and two of his servants in north Donegal in 1878. On the Adair estate alone, there were three murders in the 1860s, of which the Murray murder was the first. County Donegal itself was one of the worst counties in the country for agrarian crime of all kinds; if the thirty-two counties are ranked according to frequency of agrarian crime, Donegal was eighth in the decade 1851–60, and eleventh in 1861–70.[42]

The Irish constabulary, whose duty it was to apprehend the perpetrators of crime, including agrarian crime, were frequently criticized for their incompetence. In 1859 a judge at the summer assizes in the King's County, declared he did not 'know the purpose for which a police force is organized, if it be not to prevent crime and outrage ...but with respect to the results... they have been such as if the duty had not been performed at all'.[43] The military character of the force was criticized because it reduced their efficiency as policemen. When in 1862 three landlords were murdered, all within a period of four months and all in broad daylight, the grand jury of Tipperary forwarded a resolution to the Irish government criticizing the heavy, military accoutrements of the constabulary: 'their recent equipment with a heavy and delicate weapon, such as the rifle and sword-bayonet, rendered it impossible for them to pursue a delinquent over a close or hilly country'.[44]

The constabulary had a detective force of so-called 'disposables' who were, according to the inspector general of the force, 'always ready to mount the frieze, to assume the short pipe, to converse (many of them) in the Irish language, and to employ devices, as an Irishman knows how, to come at the knowledge they are in quest of'.[45] They were, however, so 'strictly cautioned against anything like a system of espionage', that they were, according to one bitter critic, as well known to the people as their parish priest. This same critic dismissed the whole constabulary as 'greatly overrated since the Tipperary cabbage-garden business, when they were given the credit of quashing Smith O'Brien's abortion'.[46]

Adair was able to represent himself as a protector of public order and the rights of property, encouraged by the fierce partisanship of some newspapers. When the rector of Gartan, Henry Maturin, joined the local catholic priest in begging Adair, in an open letter, to spare the people, one newspaper sarcastically dismissed the rector with the following remarkable piece of abuse: 'no man educated in Trinity College could have had anything to do with the composition of such a document'.[47] Nor was Adair slow to put his case before the public in letters to the newspapers and in a printed statement. He attempted to justify the evictions by claiming that he acted as he did because he had incurred the hatred of the Ribbonmen in County Donegal: 'What course was left to me? I offered to abandon these evictions with pleasure, if government could give me any assurance or guarantee for the safety of myself or my servants.' Adair produced a long list of depredations committed against himself and his property: he had been physically attacked by the Derryveagh people while shooting on the mountains; 'upwards of 600' of his sheep had been destroyed; the car-owners in Church Hill refused to hire their vehicles to him from 'dread of the Ribbon system'; his steward had been murdered; an attempt had been made to burn down the rectory while he was staying there; two members of the coroner's jury that brought in the verdict of murder on Murray were attacked; his dogs had been poisoned; the Derryveagh people, after Murray's murder, mockingly said that 'the fairies came out of the rocks and killed him'.

4 Post-famine clearances

The argument that the evictions exemplified the weaknesses of the Irish land system seemed a sound one to contemporaries. As with so much public debate in Ireland at that time, the evictions were immediately assimilated to existing controversies, and used merely to illustrate propositions or to expand arguments already formulated. The actual problems of estate management and law enforcement were less clearly understood than the certainty engendered by partisanship suggested. A closer look at the murder of James Murray and the subsequent evictions—a closer look, certainly, than that taken by many contemporaries—suggests that the evictions were no more typical of ordinary relations between landlords and tenants than the murder of James Murray was typical of agrarian crime in particular or rural crime in general.

Evictions like those at Derryveagh—the simultaneous removal from one estate of 47 families and the levelling of 28 houses—were rare, if not unique, after the early 1850s. During the post-famine years evictions were numerous—about 45,000 families were evicted in the five-year period 1849–53—but numbers fell rapidly after that. Between 1854 and 1878 the number of families annually evicted exceeded 1,000 in only four years: 1,817 in 1854; 1,348 in 1855; 1,522 in 1863; and 1,590 in 1864. (It is possible to account for all four of these years: the relatively high figures in 1854 and 1855 seem to be the end of the famine evictions; the high figures for 1863–4 were caused by a series of bad seasons in the early 1860s.) The number of houses levelled—a better indicator of a clearance such as Derryveagh where 28 houses were levelled—did not exceed 200 a year in the whole country after 1856 and was usually less than 100. Considering that there were over 500,000 holdings in Ireland and almost 800,000 houses in rural areas, an annual eviction rate of 1,000 families and the levelling of 100 houses was modest. In County Donegal the number of houses levelled exceeded 10 in only two years after 1854: 38 in 1861, of which 28 were at Derryveagh, and 13 in 1868. The effect of the Derryveagh evictions on the annual eviction returns for Donegal was to produce a dramatic increase in 1860 and 1861 compared with the preceding and succeeding years.[48] A careful examination of the annual returns for other counties reveals only a handful of similar cases, if the general increase in evictions in most counties in the early 1860s is ignored; the most dramatic case was that of King's County in 1857 when 242 evictions were reported, compared with 9 in the previous year and 38 in the next year.[49] None of these cases was accompanied by the levelling of houses associated with the evictions in County Donegal in 1861, suggesting that whatever their causes, they were not similar in all respects to the Derryveagh evictions. (It is worth noting that the increase in evictions in the King's County in 1857 was almost certainly caused by the breaking of 110 leases on the Digby estate by Adair's uncle, William Steuart Trench.)[50]

Compared with some of the post-famine clearances, Derryveagh was a small affair; in 1851, for example, 267 houses were levelled on the Martin estate in County Galway and 164 on the Lucan estate in County Mayo; in that same year, there were over fifty clearances as serious as that at Derryveagh ten years later.[51] But Derryveagh was a striking event in 1861: there had been nothing quite like it for a number of years; evictions as a whole were steadily declining; eviction, for the most part, was a form of insolvency, a fate suffered by tenants who could not pay their rents. The typical eviction after the early 1850s was that of the individual tenant who could not pay his rent or who consistently caused trouble on an estate. It was mainly a fate suffered by individuals and not by groups. The real problem of estate management was not the sweeping away of whole communities or the capricious eviction of solvent, improving tenants, as many contemporaries believed, but the inevitable removal of the feckless, the unfortunate and the unviable. The main cause of evictions was not landlords like Adair but falling agricultural prices or poor harvests: the periods of highest eviction figures—the early 1850s, the early 1860s and the late 1870s—were also periods of depression in agriculture and of accumulating arrears of rent. Not the least of Derryveagh's significance was to create a misleading impression of what was wrong with the land system, an impression that was turned into legislative reality in the land act of 1870, which was cleverly and effectively designed to prevent a recurrence of Derryveagh. The more important problem—the insolvency of large numbers of tenants in bad years—was virtually ignored until the outbreak of the land war in 1879.

5 Agrarian crime

If Irish landlords rarely evicted their tenants in large numbers, the murder of Murray, when similarly placed in its statistical context, turns out to have been no more typical of ordinary landlord-tenant relations than the simultaneous eviction of 47 families. In so far as one can trust the statistics of crime so meticulously compiled by the police, and they are no more misleading than contemporaries' impressions of what was happening, Ireland was not greatly more violent or crime-ridden, as far as serious crime was concerned, than England and Wales. Comparing the two parts of the United Kingdom in the 1860s— Ireland with England and Wales—Ireland had, on the basis of population, fewer indictable offences, although the frequency of certain serious crimes varied from country to country. The Irish were just as likely as the English and Welsh to commit murder, attempted murder, manslaughter and rape; the Irish, were, however, more likely to assault each other, to assault the police, to be drunk and disorderly, to expose themselves indecently and to kill and maim cattle; but they were less likely to be cruel to animals, to assault women and children, to assault with intent to ravish and abuse, to commit acts of sodomy and bestiality, and to break the game laws.[52] It is worth noting, too, that the Irish constabulary were as effective as the locally controlled forces in England and Wales: in most years in the 1860s, a slightly higher percentage of serious crimes were prosecuted to conviction than in England and Wales.

A comparison of petty crime—that disposed of summarily before justices of the peace—shows, however, that Ireland was much more disorderly than England and Wales. But this does not demonstrate conclusively that Ireland was a crime-ridden society; for it is possible that, to some extent at least, the difference between Ireland and England and Wales was more apparent than real. When comparing crime in different areas, even areas in a common legislative area such as the United Kingdom in the nineteenth century, it is difficult to go beyond comparisons of the simplest kind, limited to the incidence of those crimes most difficult to conceal or to invent, such as murder. The proportion of total crime actually observed and recorded by the police depends on the numbers of the police, the moral values of the public, the political needs of the government, the relationship between the police, the government and important groups such as local gentry, and the tendency of individuals to use the police in carrying on quarrels with their neighbours. While it is difficult to be certain about all aspects of the relationship between police and society in Ireland, it seems that there was a tendency for crime to be more thoroughly reported, if not actually exaggerated, than in other parts of the United Kingdom. As the inspector general noted ruefully, both the quantity and seriousness of criminal acts were inflated by the public; for example, 'every burning in this country, with very few exceptions, is called malicious'.[53] The reasons for this tendency were collectively obvious, if imprecise in their individual influence. There were, for example, at least twice as many police per 10,000 of the population in Ireland as in England and Wales; the Irish force was more strictly controlled by the central government, more uniform in its procedures, more coherent in its ethos, than the English and Welsh forces; as a statistics collecting machine, the Irish constabulary were unique in the United Kingdom, highly experienced and widely employed; local people were not reluctant to involve police and magistrates in their quarrels with each other; many of the most frequently reported crimes were of a public and easily detectable character, such as drunken brawls.

The combined influence of all these circumstances may explain the great amount of trivial crime recorded in Ireland; just as the relative infrequency of infractions of the game laws in Ireland—England's 'agrarian crime'—may have been caused by the relative fewness of gamekeepers in Ireland.[54] Comparisons of the incidence of crime are best confined to those crimes which were not only difficult to conceal but also difficult to invent: murder, manslaughter, serious assaults. The impression that the incidence of these was about the same in both countries is confirmed by one other crude indicator of serious crime, the number of hangings; in three years in the mid-1860s, for example, there were 29 in England and Wales and 8 in Ireland—rather fewer in Ireland than the relative population of the two would suggest. (In the same period, in the provinces of Victoria and New South Wales, whose combined populations were about a quarter of Ireland's, there were 27 hangings, including one for sodomy.[55])

Agrarian crime, which attracted so much public attention and which was classified separately from 'ordinary' crime, was without any statistical equivalent in the rest of the United Kingdom, although as a category it exists and is easily identified in any rural society.[56] As a category of Irish crime, however, agrarian crime accounted for only about, at most, 10 per cent of all crime, except in periods of great tension such as the land war, 1879–82, when, of course, it accounted for a very high proportion of all crime. The significance of agrarian crime as a component of all crime was, in practice, less than a mere comparison of the numbers of each would suggest: the most commonly recorded agrarian crime was the trivial, but alarming, sending of threatening letters; the next most common, malicious burnings, was also likely to be exaggerated in its incidence by the public, since compensation could be claimed from the county for property maliciously destroyed. In practice, from the point of view of law enforcement and the safety of life and property in the countryside, the two most serious agrarian crimes were murder and the conspiracy among the tenants known as Ribbonism.

It is tempting to dismiss the Ribbon society as a phantom of police mythology, at most a generic term for a *modus operandi* among disgruntled tenants. The account of the Ribbon 'trial' in Trench's *Realities of Irish life* is too good a story, with its drunkenness, historical bombast, and the shrewd suggestion by one of the Ribbon leaders, that the agent, condemned to death in the course of the night's potations, should not be 'put off the walk' until he had given him two iron gates promised some time before.[57] (When 'fact' in mid-nineteenth-century Ireland resembles the fiction of Carleton and Lever rather than that of Trollope, it should be distrusted.) Police and magistrates were often sceptical of the existence of such conspiracies; in 1862, for example, a Donegal magistrate, George Frazer Brady of Bunbeg, who was also Lord George Hill's agent, received information that a secret society called 'Molly's men' met in a certain public house and were armed with pistols; but the R.M. was sceptical, believing that the informant did not have 'any information to give, but is rather playing on the credulity of Mr Brady who is agent to Lord George Hill, on whose estate [he lives]'. The R.M. went on, however, to say that 'Ribbonism has existed in all parts of this county, yet in consequence of the convictions had at the recent assizes, followed by such deservedly severe punishments it will, I apprehend, be some time before it rears its head again'.[58]

He seems to have been alluding to an incident that took place in the same year as the events at Derryveagh. In November 1861, Head Constable Byrne of Letterkenny went to the public house of Anne McDevitt in that town and arrested, after a struggle, four men whom he suspected of being Ribbonmen. One of them, Denis MacMenemin tried to destroy some papers before he was arrested; when these were pieced together by the police, they revealed passwords and the names of Ribbon leaders in Sligo, Enniskillen, Cootehill, Belfast, Castlewellan, Clough and Newcastle-on-Tyne; when these were investigated by the local police they were found to be, in fact, men who had long been suspected of Ribbonism. Head Constable Byrne had stumbled on a conspiracy with extensive ramifications not only in the north of Ireland but among the Irish in the north of England as well. This view of the Ribbon movement was strengthened by the fact that after the arrests in Letterkenny 'subscriptions to a very large amount' were collected to retain legal advisers for the defendants; also, when they were remanded on bail, it was, according to the R.M., 'very significant' to see the alacrity with which bailsmen presented themselves.[59] The possession of such documents was not enough, however, to establish the guilt of the accused; but conclusive evidence was provided several weeks later by an informer, 'a labouring man', who had been a Ribbon-man for six years. He was able not only to give the police the names of all the Ribbonmen around Ballybofey but also stated on oath that Denis MacMenemin had told him that he had been a Ribbon 'delegate' for eighteen years. The police were at pains to assure the authorities in Dublin Castle that this information was freely given: the informant had not been threatened by the police or offered any inducement but had acted as he did because he was 'very much annoyed with the society for not bailing him'.[60]

One of the most complete descriptions of Ribbonism was compiled by the police in the 1880s. A hierarchy of county delegates, parish masters, 'body masters', committee men and 'mere' Ribbonmen existed in the counties of Leitrim, Longford, Meath, Westmeath, Louth, Cavan, Monaghan, Armagh, Fermanagh, Tyrone and Donegal. The first three groups in the hierarchy—the county delegates, parish masters and body masters—were the directors and supervisors of the movement; the committee men were the actual perpetrators of the crimes of revenge decreed by the leaders, paying 6d. a quarter for access to passwords; the 'mere' Ribbonmen were probationers who would be admitted to full membership when they had distinguished themselves 'by acts of outrage, waylaying, malicious injury to property etc'. The aims of the society were as comprehensive as its organization was hierarchical: to shoot and destroy all protestant or heretic landlords or employers; to burn down or sack protestant churches; to defend 'the farmer, the poor man, the widow and orphans of any brother, or former brother against the oppression of the landlords and the tyranny of Saxon laws'; and 'to procure the independence of Ireland'.[61]

From the mass of contradictory accounts of Ribbonism, it is possible to come to some tentative conclusions about its prevalence. First, some form of conspiratorial confederacy, wider than groups of townlands or parishes, probably did exist, but was probably declining in this period. Secondly, Ribbonism, whatever its antagonism to landlords, was not exclusively, or even mainly, a tenant organization; of the twelve conspirators named by the informant at Ballybofey, there were six labourers, a baker, a butcher, a publican, a tailor and two with no specified occupations.[62] Thirdly, in spite of the sanguinary sectarianism of their oath, the Ribbonmen did not kill many of their enemies, either landlords or employers; very few murders when investigated turned out to be Ribbon executions. Fourthly, Ribbonism as a permanent, standing conspiracy, jealously watching the actions of landlords and agents, did not exist in every parish. When landlords outraged the feelings of their tenants, resistance was spontaneously organized; the resistance to William Scully at Ballycohey in County Tipperary in 1868, when Scully, his bailiff and a police escort were met with a hail of gun-fire as they tried to evict tenants, was, according to the police, not the work of 'an organized and secret society', but the work of the people of the townland who had suddenly organized themselves.[63]

It is doubtful if Ribbonism existed in Gartan and Derryveagh before, or even after, the Derryveagh evictions; in the police reports there was no hint that the murder of Murray was a Ribbon outrage, except in the information of William Deery, who was later convicted of perjury. If Adair encountered a combination among his tenants, it was spontaneous, based on ties of kinship and a common feeling of insecurity. It was predictable, however, that the nephew of William Steuart Trench should imagine that any resistance to his will was traceable to schemes hatched in the small hours, aided by deep potations of illicitly distilled whiskey.

Agrarian homicides, that is murders and manslaughters committed in connection with disputes about the tenure of land, were the most serious part of agrarian crime; but such homicides were relatively rare—about 6 per cent of all homicides—and what is just as important, and more revealing, only a quarter of all agrarian homicides were caused by disputes between landlords and tenants. It is easy to be misled by the term 'agrarian crime', which implies that a whole category of crime was caused by disputes between landlords and tenants; but an examination of individual crimes shows that the police included rows between tenants about trespassing, family disputes about inheritance and quarrels over rights of way, as well as landlord–tenant disputes. The belief that it was dangerous to be an Irish landlord was grossly exaggerated: nine landlords, one agent, seven bailiffs and ten other servants of landlords were killed in the period 1857–78; but seven of these were accounted for by only three incidents: two murders on the Adair estate in 1860 and 1863, two at Ballycohey in 1868 and the murder of Lord Leitrim and two servants in 1878. If this sounds impressive, it was not when set against all crime in general and homicides in particular: 27 homicides involving landlords and their servants must be set against almost 2,000 homicides of all kinds during the same period. Confining the comparison to agrarian homicides, three tenants or members of tenants' families were killed for every landlord or landlord's servant in disputes about land. In County Donegal itself, the scene of the most dramatic murder of a landlord in the second half of the nineteenth century, agrarian homicides were caused mainly by family disputes and disputes between tenants: of the twelve agrarian homicides between 1857 and 1878, Adair's servants Murray and Grierson, and Lord Leitrim and his two servants, accounted for five; the remainder were caused by disputes between tenants or family rows, including a case of matricide in 1867 and a fight in 1875 where one of the parties 'died from the effects of a bite in the thumb'.[64]

It was probably more dangerous to be an Irish landlord than an English one; but, on the other hand, it was probably more dangerous to be an English gamekeeper than an Irish bailiff. But Irish landlords were not extremely at risk: it was more dangerous to work on the Irish railways, to ride to foxhounds, or to be a member of a European royal house—Queen Victoria was attacked more frequently, if with less effect, than Lord Leitrim. The incidence and importance of agrarian crime were greatly exaggerated; at most it was the adjunct of rural disorder as a whole. The abolition of landlordism, or its transformation by legislative restictions, would have reduced total crime by only 3 or 4 per cent. Agrarian crimes attracted attention because they were sensational rather than significant. Their importance was exaggerated by their connection with a great public controversy; they seemed to be preventable, either by legislation limiting landlords' powers, or by more ruthless law enforcement; the circumstances surrounding the murder of a landord or an agent were more complicated, had more ramifications and presented more opportunities for journalistic reporting than common, domestic murders; also, the exalted position of some of the victims ensured a prurient curiosity that was as common among Victorians as it is today. When such sensational incidents are set against the background of all crime in Ireland, they lose much of their significance; only when it is assumed that they occurred either in a vacuum, or in an otherwise peaceful countyside, do they stand out.

6 Murray's murderers are not detected

The argument that the murder of James Murray and the eviction of 47 families were too unusual to be regarded as anything more than a most extreme example of a quarrel between a landlord and his tenants can be supported by statistics of evictions and agrarian crimes. The argument can be taken further by the detailed records of the transaction kept by police and magistrates. A large file was built up in the chief secretary's office by the diligence of Sir Thomas Larcom, the under-secretary, responding to pressure from Vincent Scully, M.P. for County Cork, who brought the case before the house of commons. These papers, especially one removed from the file and included in his own papers by Larcom,[65] reveal that the evictions were exceptional not only statistically; they were part of a drama whose unfolding owed little to the tensions normally associated with the management of estates.

Adair's charges against his tenants were carefully investigated by the police with interesting results; for Adair was either a liar or careless about details. His sheep had not been killed by his tenants but by his own shepherds; an attempt had not been made to burn down the rectory while he was staying there—the rector later told the police that careless servant girls had probably started a fire while milking cows; the attack on him while shooting on the mountains was not the fault of the Derryveagh tenants, but was provoked by his own arrogance; one of the coroner's jury at Murray's inquest had been assaulted but the assault arose from a quarrel in which his servant had been involved; Murray's successor as steward had been assaulted but only as a result of his own intervention in a drunken quarrel; nor had Adair's dogs been poisoned maliciously.

It is possible that Adair was genuinely mistaken about the character of his tenants, or carried away by emotion; it is also possible that he was the dupe of his own servants. The affair of the missing sheep, 16 of whose hides were found in Murray's house, suggests that Murray was not above cheating his master as well as the ratepayers. Adam Grierson, Murray's successor, was also capable of deceiving Adair: after the evictions, for example, he wrote to Adair telling him that 'there were no houses knocked down', but the police report of the evictions stated that 28 houses were unroofed or levelled.

Both the protestant rector and the poor-law authorities believed that the Derryveagh people were 'a superior class of people'; the rector told the police that he never locked his doors at night. A return of crimes reported in the barony of Kilmacrenan in the ten years 1851–61 showed that the rector was not behaving foolishly, for Gartan was one of the most peaceful parishes in the barony: in ten years a horse and a cow had been stolen; a man had been accused of 'giving medicine to cause an abortion' to a daughter of one of the Derryveagh tenants; a few threatening letters had been received; the most serious crime, apart from those involving Adair and his servants, was the burning of an out-house and eight cattle in May 1860 in 'a family dispute'.[66] The seven magistrates from Church Hill who met at Letterkenny in March 1861 to pass a resolution condemning Adair were exaggerating only slightly when they claimed that their estates were in 'a state of perfect tranquillity'. Adair's allegation that his tenants were disorderly, violent, and murderous conspirators came to depend more and more on his belief that they had murdered his steward; what had been the gravamen of his case in early 1861 became, in the face of vigorous investigation and contradiction by the police, his whole case by April 1861.

The murder of Murray was the most mysterious, as well as the most important, charge against the tenants; the police quickly disposed of the other charges, but they did not succeed in identifying and bringing to trial Murray's murderers. The investigation of the case passed through several stages before the police admitted failure. Acting on information elicited at Murray's inquest and later before the magistrates, the police at first suspected Manus Rodden and the

Sweeneys of Derryveagh. Dugald Rankin, one of Adair's Scots shepherds, who lived as a lodger with Murray and his wife, testified that Murray had quarrelled with the Sweeneys about trespassing; a local man, Patrick Ward from Derryveagh, had seen Manus Rodden cutting hazel rods on the mountain, and cut rods were found near the scene of the murder; footprints at the scene of the murder corresponded with the 'highlow' shoes worn by Rodden. The Sweeneys' house was searched and a shirt and other pieces of cloth stained with blood were found; an examination by a doctor in Dublin revealed in one of the cloths 'the presence of blood cells possessing the configuration, and falling within the micrometric range of human blood'. The police's suspicion that the Sweeneys had been in a fight was confirmed by the fact that one of them had a black eye that he claimed he had got building a corn stack. Mary, Donald, and James Sweeney were arrested and remanded in custody. The police were sure they had the culprits because Edward Sweeney, Mary's father, told a policeman that his daughter 'could tell all if she liked, but that she was very sulky'. Eventually the case against the Sweeneys and Rodden collapsed for want of further evidence; the Sweeneys were discharged and Rodden was released on bail. The most interesting aspect of this stage of the investigation—apart from the crudeness of the medical evidence on the blood stains, which cost the government 15 guineas—was the remarkably clear, detailed, and acute evidence given by Dugald Rankin, who showed powers of observation and deduction that would have graced the pages of Sir Arthur Conan Doyle.

The next stage of the inquiry was determined by the evidence of William Deery, a discharged soldier who had served in the Land Transport Corps in the Crimea and later in the militia. Deery claimed not only to know the workings of the Ribbon society in north Donegal, but also the identity of Murray's murderers and of the man who attempted to murder Rev. Alexander Nixon in October 1858. According to him, the Ribbonmen recognized each other by secret signs such as 'raising the covering off the head and turning the little finger to the hair, as if scratching it'; Rev. Alexander Nixon had been shot by a man named Foy, then employed in Glasgow; Murray had been attacked by a crowd of 120 and beaten to death, having shot a man named Bradley before he was overpowered.

The fourteen named by Deery were arrested, including the

unfortunate Foy, who was brought back in police custody from Glasgow where he seems to have had a steady job. But Deery's evidence was defective: when brought to the scene of Murray's murder he could not point out the place of the murder; he claimed that Murray was wearing a 'Tom and Jerry' hat when attacked, but the police knew he had been wearing a cap; the presence of 120 people on the mountain when Murray was murdered was impossible since the footprints of only three assailants had been discovered. The man Bradley, who was supposed to have been shot by Murray, was not known to the police and was not one of the Bradleys of Derryveagh; Foy, whose demeanour had been so promising when confronted with Deery— 'appealing to him for mercy, but denying the charge'—was cleared when a telegram to his employer in Glasgow confirmed that he had been there on the day of the attack on Rev. Alexander Nixon. The crown solicitor, having come to the conclusion that Deery was 'a man of bad character amongst the people, and would not have been trusted by them', ordered the release of the suspects, and the papers of the case were sent to the attorney general to prosecute Deery for perjury.

It was at this point, early in February 1861, that Adair initiated legal proceedings to enforce the notices to quit that had expired the previous November. The failure of the police to detect Murray's murderers and the apparent complicity of the Derryveagh tenants were his excuse for removing forcibly tenants who had given up possession on the understanding that they would be readmitted as tenants when the boundaries of their holdings had been rearranged.

The failure of the police to apprehend the murderers was easily explained in terms other than the silence of the tenants, one of whom at least was willing to give evidence against his neighbours. Crude detection techniques—blood tests, for example, that could only with difficulty establish the presence of human blood in a blood-stained garment—prevented the police from establishing the guilt of suspects indicated by circumstantial evidence; the scene of the crime, a remote and deserted mountain in a wild area, made it unlikely that anyone had witnessed the murder or seen suspects on their way to or from it. In the absence of eye-witnesses able to name the culprits, or suspects willing to confess, there was not much that the police could do except follow the unreliable lead of a rascal like William Deery in the hope that something would turn up. Nor could the police use the trick, even if they had thought of it, of playing one faction against another because the Derryveagh tenants, isolated along the lake and cut off by the mountains, seem to have been a closely knit community.

Just after the evictions in April, the rector of Gartan, Rev. Henry Maturin, hinted publicly that the failure of the police might have another cause: they had not directed their attention to the right group of suspects. In an open letter to Adair, he tried to exculpate the tenants: 'What would be Mr Adair's feelings, if it were found out hereafter that the murder was committed by persons in no way connected with the Derryveagh tenantry, now exterminated on account of it, and whose wailings might then, without avail, for ever ring in his ears?'

7 Who murdered Murray?

The circumstances of Murray's death were capable of an explanation that did not involve the tenants. Murray had always gone out armed; since his early quarrels with the tenants, he had gone in fear of his life; yet he was killed with a blow from a large stone on an open mountain where assailants could not easily have surprised him. He had fired only one shot from his revolver, 'the revolving apparatus having been, or become deranged'; the lining of his pocket was turned inside out, suggesting that either he had difficulty in pulling out his gun, or did so in a hurry. The circumstances of the murder, therefore, suggest that Murray was murdered by men whom he did not regard as enemies; a timorous, even a prudent man, would have had his gun at the ready, if approached by men whom he feared in such an isolated area.

Also, why did his revolver jam after the first shot? Dugald Rankin, who gave such clear evidence at the inquest, said he had discharged Murray's gun the night before he disappeared; but Murray, he said, had reloaded it the next morning before setting out. Robert Kerr, a gamekeeper, told the magistrates that the revolver had jammed because a ball had protruded beyond the revolving chamber and prevented the magazine from rotating. He did not explain how this could have happened, nor did the police and magistrates show any interest in the question. It is possible that Murray loaded his gun carelessly; it is also possible that the ball just worked itself loose—a common accident in some revolvers. It is also possible that the gun had been tampered with, although it must be admitted that the method was such a crude one that it could have been easily detected; moreover, such a method of jamming, if done by someone who hoped to be able to attack Murray with impunity, would not have prevented the chamber under the hammer from discharging effectively. If Murray were attacked by men who he thought were friends, it is possible that they tampered with his gun *after* he was murdered, in order to create the impression that a violent struggle had taken place. Revolvers in use in 1860s, such as Col. Colt's or Messrs Deane & Adams', had detachable magazines: Murray's murderers could have come equipped with a spare magazine, one chamber of which had been discharged and another fitted with a badly placed ball; after the murder, the spare magazine would have been substituted for the magazine from which no shots had been fired.

It is possible to reconstruct Murray's murder on the basis of two facts: that he must have been attacked by men whom he did not regard as enemies; that he was attacked by men who did not fear his revolver. The aim of his assailants was to create a convincing *mise en scene*: an attack that looked spontaneous and crude, suggesting a frenzied assault by wild peasants, goaded to fury on the spur of the moment and succeeding only because the victim's revolver jammed in the heat of action. A further advantage for the planners was, of course, that no shot was actually fired, so there was no startling sound to attract attention; nor was there any possibility that the assailants, if seen in the area, could have been proved to have been there at the exact time of Murray's murder, since the time of the attack could have been established only by reference to the sound of a gunshot.

An alternative explanation based on these principles, but not on these lines, was put forward less than ten years after the murder by Patrick Sarsfield Cassidy in *Glenveigh, or the victims of vengeance*, published in Boston in 1870. Cassidy, who was born at Dunkineely but spent his early years with his uncle at Church Hill, may or may not have been repeating local rumours, current at the time of the murder and familiar to local people. What is clear, however, is that Cassidy was scurrilously outspoken and did not fear the penalties of the civil law. He claimed that the murder had been planned by Adair himself and executed by his bastard son Bob, and his steward Adam Grierson. (Throughout the text of the novel, Cassidy referred to Adair as 'Adams', not for reasons of delicacy or fear of a libel suit, but for 'the simple reason my pen positively refused to write the real one'.) Adair's motive for murdering Murray was pecuniary; Murray had a lease for 21 years, 19 of which were unexpired, and another Scotsman had offered Adair a higher rent. Also, Adair hoped that in the outcry after the murder, he would be able to 'sweep the scum of wretched animals, who encumber my property, off it'. Bob's motive was rather more immediate: he had been whipped by Murray for paying attentions to Mrs Murray. Bob and his accomplice, Grierson, planned to beat Murray to death with the butts of their guns to make it appear that the tenants had done it. In the event they shot him from a range of ten yards and then beat in his head. The results were as Adair hoped: an innocent man was accused of the murder; the evictions took place, carried out by a crowbar brigade of 100 Glaswegians, protected by 500 police.

After the evictions, the story culminates in the murder of Grierson by Bob, again at the instigation of Adair who wanted rid of Grierson; the murder of Grierson is fathered on the innocent Francis Bradley by the false testimony of Mrs Eliza Campbell, whose husband had succeeded Grierson as steward. (Mrs Campbell had, of course, succeeded Mrs Murray as the irrepressible Bob's paramour.) The story ends with Francis Bradley's acquittal at the assizes, thanks to the stirring oratory of a great barrister, thus escaping the embarassment of adding to the troubles of the sub-sheriff, Samuel Crookshank, by a mutually distressing *rencontre* on the scaffold before Lifford jail. Finally, Adair leaves County Donegal 'to travel on the Continent ... his unwieldy and corrupt body fast becoming literally eaten away by a combination of the most loathsome diseases'.[67]

Cassidy's novel was not one of the great works of Victorian fiction; nor was it a completely accurate historical account. There is, for example, no evidence for the existence of 'Bob'; nor was Murray a tenant with a lease, for he was clearly Adair's steward. On one major point, however, Cassidy knew what he was talking about, for the police and magistrates seem to have come slowly to the conclusion that Murray's murderers were not to be found among the Derryveagh tenants. The third set of suspects who attracted the police's attention were less interesting than Cassidy's, but it is their existence that makes the whole affair so remarkable, reinforcing the argument that this was not a typical quarrel between a landlord and his tenants. Near the end of May 1861, nearly two months after the evictions, Vincent Scully, M.P. for County Cork, who had brought the evictions to the attention of the house of commons, wrote to the chief secretary claiming that Murray had been murdered by his lodger, Dugald Rankin, and that he could supply enough evidence to hang him. Larcom the under-secretary was sceptical but on further inquiry, Theobald Dillon, one of the R.M.s involved in the case, gave what seems to have been the final police opinion on the murder of Murray: 'I believe that [Mrs Murray] and Dugald Rankin conspired to get Murray murdered, and I believe the actual murderer was Archibald Campbell, one of the late Mr Hunter's shepherds, who perjured himself before Chief Justice Monahan'.

The motive was a predictable one; on one occasion, as early as March 1861, Adam Grierson was in the kitchen of Glenveagh Cottage with Mrs Murray 'when Rankin came in and he remarked that a very cold and distant salute passed between them. He got up and left, closing the door after him, but suddenly re-entered and found them kissing, locked in each other's arms.' Their liaison went back further than March when Grierson found them together. According to the police, whose vigorous prurience more than compensated for their lack of scientific techniques of detection, Mrs Murray, on the morning of Murray's disappearance, refused to give him milk for his porridge. 'There is only a little there and I am keeping if for Rankin and the devil a drop of it you shall get.' This could have been the solicitude of a kindly landlady for her lodger's comfort; but the police were also able to report that Rankin and Mrs Murray were sharing the same bedroom just after Murray's funeral. The police case against Rankin was not only the fact that he was Mrs Murray's lover; more importantly, they discovered that he had been careful to establish an alibi for himself on the day of the murder; also, he had been seen frequently in the company of Campbell, the actual murderer.

The evidence against Rankin, Mrs Murray, and Campbell was not conclusive and the police did not proceed against them; but the evidence against them was as strong as against Manus Rodden and the Sweeneys. Both groups had motives: on the one hand, violent revenge for deeply felt wrongs; on the other, the dissolution of an inconvenient marriage; also, both groups had the opportunity to commit the murder. The other pieces of evidence are equally balanced: the blood-stained cloths found in the Sweeneys' house could as easily be regarded as exculpatory as incriminating; Rankin's staying around Murray's house on the day of the murder could have been for purposes other than the fabrication of an alibi. What is clear, however, is that Rankin was quite capable of organizing the murder; his evidence at the inquest showed that he had an eye for detail and a sharper mind than the police and magistrates. He was capable of planning the murder in such a way as to make it appear that the tenants had done it; even the elaborate ruse of tampering with Murray's revolver by substituting one magazine for another would not have been beyond him.

The balance of probability is, in the absence of conclusive evidence, about even between the two groups of suspects, and certainty about the identity of the murderers is impossible on the basis of the surviving evidence. If the Scots criminal law had been introduced into Donegal with Scots sheep, a verdict of 'not proven' would not have been inappropriate. What is certain is that Adair's justification for the eviction of a whole community—their supposed complicity in the murder of Murray—was critically weakened by even a prima facie case against his own servants. Did Adair know that Rankin and Mrs Murray were lovers? There is no direct evidence that he did; but his steward knew of the liaison as early as March 1861; the police suspected its existence earlier; the rector of Gartan seems to have known at the time of the evictions. If Adair was ignorant, he did not remain in ignorance for long. In the house of commons on 24 June 1861, J. F. Maguire, the member for Dungarvan, claimed that 'there was one man in Donegal who was openly suspected of the crime. Whether he was guilty or not was a matter between God and himself, but it was a curious fact that this man wore the dead man's clothes at his funeral, that he was extremely intimate with the dead man's wife.'[68]

It is possible that Adair was misled by his servants and that he was as much their dupe and victim as the Derryveagh tenants. But by April 1861 Adair could have had no illusions about the character of his Scots servants: in March Rankin shot and wounded a policeman in a drunken brawl in Strabane; in April Grierson was sentenced to one month's imprisonment for assault. It is also possible that Adair knew the truth and used the murder as a pretext for doing what he had always intended: to evict tenants whose land he wanted for a sheep-farm. The inaccuracy or falsehood of so many of his statements suggest the R.M., J. S. Macleod, was not exaggerating when he claimed that 'Mr Adair will *say anything* just as it suits his purpose'. It is also possible that he was simply angry and high-handed; having convinced himself that Ribbonism had a footing on his estate, he could have fitted all his misfortunes into a consistent pattern—even the accusations against Rankin and Mrs Murray could have been dismissed as the continuation of the war against him by other means. The most telling comment on Adair's behaviour, enhanced by its freedom from rancour, came in the house of commons from Lord Palmerston, who was not a sentimentalist in his attitudes to Irish tenants: 'A man's mind must, indeed, be very much distorted who can fancy it a real justification for sweeping away a whole population that he thought they ought to give evidence against a murderer, when probably they know no more about the deed than he did himself.'[69]

8 The effects of the evictions

What permanent effects did the Derryveagh evictions have on relations between landlords and tenants, especially in County Donegal? Their role in A. M. Sullivan's history of his own times was obvious: Derryveagh marked a stage in the oppression of Irish tenants, filling a gap between the famine clearances and the land act of 1870; as well as making a good story, they contrasted with and justified the armed resistance to evictions at Ballycohey in County Tipperary in August 1868, when William Scully, the landlord, was badly wounded and his bailiff and a policeman killed.[70] The Ballycohey tragedy 'passed the land act of 1870 ... evictions of the old character and extent will henceforth hardly be attempted'.[71] (The connection between Derryveagh and Ballycohey was also seen by Cassidy: the dozen bullets fired there did more for tenant-right than all the orators.[72])

It is doubtful if Derryveagh was as important as A. M. Sullivan believed: it was not followed by a powerful parliamentary campaign to secure a measure of land reform; nor was there a great outbreak of rural disorder in the 1860s. Agrarian crime did increase slightly in the early 1860s as a result of bad seasons, but the mid-1860s were remarkably free from it. During the fenian disturbances the tenants were quiet: it was their unsympathetic attitude to fenianism that made it so easy to deal with the conspiracy; the farmers were not loyal, but they were not fenians, wishing for peace and caring little for anything but their land.[73] Two parliamentary committees investigated relations between landlords and tenants in the 1860s, but the tenants' advocates made little of the Derryveagh evictions; instead of calling Larcom, Adair, and the resident magistrates who were present at Church Hill in 1860–61, the only reference to the evictions was a passing one, and Adair was discreetly referred to as 'Mr A'.[74]

The main significance of the Derryveagh evictions in the history of the movement for reform of the land laws was that they marked one of the last flickers of life in the old 'independent' party, established in 1852 to work in parliament for a measure of security of tenure.[75] After the series of political disasters that culminated in a tory victory at the general election in Ireland in 1859, the flurry of activity associated with Derryveagh was a reassuring experience for the small group of whigs and former Young Irelanders who still acted as the tenants' spokesmen. But the evictions helped to conceal one of the realities of Irish politics: the land question had been politically dead since the mid-1850s, killed by the wave of agricultural prosperity that preceded and was greatly enhanced by the Crimean war. The land question responded to its own internal pressures that were not sensitive to the needs of politicians; from the mid-1850s to the late 1870s, those pressures were not conducive to the organization of a powerful political movement. The flurry of activity in the late 1860s, culminating in the land act of 1870, owed less to tensions between landlords and tenants than it did to an act of political resurrectionism by Gladstone.

If Derryveagh was an important incident in the careers of Vincent Scully, who put the tenants' case in parliament, and A. M. Sullivan who put their case in *The Nation*, it also revealed remorsely that the inconsistencies and hypocrisies of the 'independent' party had not been confined to Sadleir and Keogh.[76] Adair had offered himself as a tenant-right candidate to the electors of County Limerick in 1857, promising 'to act in conjunction with that party, who are pledged to withhold their support from any government, not making TENANT-RIGHT a *cabinet* measure'. Adair did not seem to think that the eviction of 25 families (10 of whom were readmitted as tenants) in 1853 on his recently acquired estate in County Tipperary was a disqualification for a tenant-right M.P.[77] Was this an example of Adair's cheek, or did he perhaps, read accurately the character of the party he was seeking to join?

When Scully attacked Adair in the house of commons in June 1861, an Irish M.P. taunted him, saying 'he thought the attack on Mr Adair might with more decency and decorum have proceeded from some other member'.[78] Parliamentary language, even in the 1860s, permitted some licence, and this taunt might have meant nothing; but George Fitzmaurice writing to Larcom in July 1861 took up the same theme: 'Mr Scully should be the last man to charge a landlord with harshness towards his tenantry as there never was a more harsh landlord than himself'. One of Scully's political problems was that he was the eldest brother of William Scully, who was the target of the emancipatory fusillade at Ballycohey and who had been sentenced to 12 months' imprisonment in 1865 for wounding the wife of a tenant whom he was trying to evict.[79] It is possible that the two men were mistakenly identified as one; Vincent, for example, complained of the carelessness of journalists who referred to his brother as 'Mr Scully', ignoring the convention that the designation 'Mr', unaccompanied by a Christian name, was reserved for the head of a family. The only reliable evidence that exists to show that the charges against Vincent Scully were true is in a police report on evictions in 1850 that shows he evicted 21 families (7 of whom were readmitted as tenants) in the south riding of Tipperary.[80] It is true that 1850 was one of the worst years for evictions, and landlords who were later held up as models of kindness evicted tenants in the terrible years after the famine; but it is also true that until the eviction of the 47 families at Derryveagh, there was not much to choose between Scully, the tenants' champion, and Adair, the rejected tenant-right candidate. If the road to the land act of 1870 started with the famine clearances and the formation of the 'independent' party in the early 1850s, and passed through Derryveagh and Ballycohey, it followed a circuitous route; those who marched to the tune of the 'Pope's Brass Band' did not march in a straight line.

What effects did the Derryveagh evictions have on relations between landlords and tenants in County Donegal? If Adair had hoped to restore order to the area by the evictions, he did not succeed. Many of the evicted tenants remained in the locality and friction between them and the Scotsmen continued. John Coyle swore at the petty sessions that he had seen Dugald Rankin killing Adair's sheep; Coyle's uncle and mother had been allowed to remain in their holding as caretakers, but when John gave information against Rankin, Grierson turned them out. (The magistrates at Church Hill referred this case to the law advisers of the crown, implying that Grierson had forged the document in which the tenants gave up possession.[81]) Grierson, who was described by the police as 'a Scotchman of a very low class ... drunken and reckless', was in trouble again later in 1861 for shooting at a tenant and beating another with a pistol. He was imprisoned for three months and his licence to carry arms revoked—a virtual sentence of death as it happened.

At some time after his release from prison, Grierson quarrelled with Adair and was dismissed. He planned to emigrate to Queensland—a good destination since many of those he evicted had already gone to New South Wales—but delayed his departure because Adair would not pay his arrears of wages or give him a reference. In April 1863, when he was returning home late one evening, he was shot and mortally wounded by an assailant whom he identified in a dying declaration as Francis Bradley, a son of one of the evicted tenants. Just before the murder, the police had searched Grierson's house for arms; they were acting on information given by Adair's servants, one of whom was described as Adair's 'confidential' housekeeper; but according to the police she occupied 'a more *tender position* in his household' than that of housekeeper. Unfortunately the file on the Grierson case was not retained in the State Paper Office, and details of his relationship with Adair remains obscure. But the fate of Bradley is well known: he was put on trial for the murder of Grierson; three juries disagreed between 1863 and 1865 and he was discharged when the Crown decided to take no further proceedings.

The history of Adair's dealings with his tenants after 1863 can be reconstructed from a few pieces of information. All but three of the families allowed to remain as caretakers or tenants at the time of the evictions were eventually removed; but the three families allowed to remain stayed there for years without disturbance. There was a report in 1863 from the R.M., J. S. Macleod, that Adair had obtained 22 ejectments at the quarter sessions but there is no evidence of a large number of evictions taking place in 1863 or later: the valuation records show that while holdings changed hands on the estate, the number and size of holdings remained virtually unchanged until the end of the century.[82] In 1866 Rev. Daniel Kair, the priest who had joined the rector in begging Adair to spare the people, took a farm of 56 acres in the townland of Kilmore, owned by Adair. If he inherited the farm, the transaction tells nothing about his opinion of Adair; but if he bought the farm under the Ulster custom, his action was a surprising vote of confidence in his landlord.

Another clue to Adair's dealings with his tenants came in 1869, when a select committee investigating the tenement valuation wandered for a minute or two from its immediate business, the questioning of Sir Richard Griffith, to discuss the Derryveagh evictions; Griffith, who had been commissioner of valuation and knew more about rural Ireland than any other man in public life, made the remarkable claim that Adair was 'now beloved by his tenants'.[83] Sir Richard was not infallible and he was an old hand at parliamentary inquiries; he was also a snob and at the end of a distinguished career in which public garrulity had played an important part; but his statement is an intriguing hint that there was a change in Adair's behaviour. But too much weight should not be attached to it. In 1868 Adair leased most of the evicted lands to two sheep-farmers, J. T. and G. M. Dixon; between 1869 and 1873, there were reports of stolen sheep and a familiar reminder of former troubles when one of the Dixons requested 'certain information' from the police about one of his shepherds.[84] (The acerbities of Adair's reign were softened by the folk memory of Cornelia, his American wife, which was benign; according to tradition, for example, 'the late Mrs Adair's father' who lived at Glenveagh Castle brought over a cargo of meal during the famine in 1847. The displacement of memory here is an interesting one: Glenveagh Castle was not built until the 1860s and Mrs Adair's father, James S. Wadsworth, was an American soldier who probably never set foot in Donegal; but the impression of benevolence is strong, if wrongly attributed.[85])

It would be unwise to set Griffith's statement against clear evidence of later troubles with sheep, but the remarkable thing about Adair's subsequent career was that he did not become embroiled in any of the major disturbances that afflicted other landlords. Although fenianism, for example, was not primarily a tenant–farmer movement, some disaffection around Church Hill would not have been surprising; but none of those arrested or suspected of fenianism in Donegal were connected with Adair's estate. Of those arrested, two came from Belleek, one from Ballyshannon; the nearest arrest was that of Michael Gallagher, a cooper in Ramelton. The fenian suspects, a much larger group than those arrested, did not include any from Church Hill. Not only did Church Hill not provide any prominent fenians, but Donegal

was one of the counties least affected by fenianism. The only connection between the Derryveagh evictions and fenianism was through the
remarkable T. N. Underwood, a barrister from Strabane, who wrote a
ballad of 13 stanzas on the evictions for Cassidy's *Glenveigh*;
according to the police, he was 'one of the principal head centres of the
fenian brotherhood'; when arrested his powers of hyperbole did not
desert him, for he told the authorities 'he could command from 10 to
12,000 men if he only raised his hand'.[86]

If the Derryveagh evictions did not contribute to the growth of
fenianism in County Donegal, one would at least expect references to
them during the land war and the plan of campaign. It is impossible to
be sure that Adair was completely untouched during the land war, but
it is clear that he did not stand out as one of its victims: in the dozens
of speeches reported by the police in County Donegal, there was not
one reference to Adair or the evictions.[87] Even Davitt in a speech in
Letterkenny in January 1881 did not refer to them, although he found
time to refer to the battle of the Boyne.[88] Father McFadden, who as a
young priest had been involved with the Derryveagh tenants, did not
even allude to Adair in his pamphlet on the land war.[89] (One of the few
references to Derryveagh in the 1880s was in a pamphlet *about* Father
McFadden.[90]) Nor was there any reference to Adair in the evidence
collected in Donegal by the Evicted Tenants' Commission; there was a
reference to his Queen's County estate where he had evicted three
tenants who were in arrears, but it was also reported that he had
reduced his rents by 15 per cent.[91]

In spite of Adair and the third earl of Leitrim, County Donegal was
relatively peaceful during the land war; when the counties of Ireland
were ranked according to their rates of agrarian crime, Donegal was
eighth and eleventh in the 1850s and 1860s; but in the ten years
1871–80 it fell to twenty-first place. As James Hack Tuke observed in
1880: 'There is a very marked change in the political and social
atmosphere of the counties of Mayo and Galway when compared with
Donegal. In the latter, with rare exceptions, there was little agitation
or openly expressed bitterness towards landlords, and the number of
police is small, and their duties not very harassing.'[92] The main anti-
landlord activity in north Donegal, apart from Lord Leitrim's murder
in April 1878, was on the Nixon, Olphert, Stewart, and Swiney estates,
neighbours of Adair, but whose contagion he escaped. In December

1881, for example, the land war came close to Adair but did not, apparently, touch him. The tenants of Mrs Stewart met their landlord at Church Hill and offered to pay their rents, reduced to Griffith's valuation; this was accepted, but after the meeting, Bryan Daly of Cabra Glebe met the tenants and 'by his interference prevented them from paying as they had agreed'.[93] Nor does Adair seem to have suffered the fate of his other neighbour Wybrants Olphert of Ballyconnel House, Falcarragh: after evicting six tenants, he was boycotted for six months in 1881 and his stables were burnt down; in 1887 his tenants demanded a rent reduction of 8s. in the pound on non-judicial rents; when this was refused, he was boycotted again.[94] Nor was Adair subject to the pressure of secret societies in the 1880s; the police report on Ribbonism in County Donegal, for example, did not mention any Ribbonmen near Church Hill.[95]

It is perhaps misleading to seek the significance of the Derryveagh evictions either in the political history of Ireland or in the history of landlord–tenant relations in Donegal. Their main significance seems to be that they were a *misleading* event in the history of the land question. When placed against evictions as a whole, and the murder of Murray put in its context, and above all, when the 'secret history' of the whole affair is revealed, neither side in the debate about Irish land could have reasonably used Derryveagh as a microcosm of the land question—the whole affair could just as plausibly be used to demonstrate the evil consequences of illicit love in a cold, wet climate.

9 Adair as a land speculator

'Mr Adair is to a great extent a dealer or speculator in land and one who would never be on good terms with the peasantry', wrote Thomas Fitzgerald, the crown solicitor of Donegal, in a letter to Sir Thomas Larcom in 1861, just after the evictions; he was repeating the common opinion that purchasers of land under the incumbered estates act were speculators who had none of the affection for their tenants shown by 'old' landlords. During the quarrels that led to the murder of Murray and the evictions, the 'old' landlords in Gartan were firmly on the side of the tenants, or at any rate, against Adair: Lt-Col. Humfrey, for example, took up the case of the men who claimed that they had been wrongfully arrested by Adair; James Johnston, who had leased Derryveagh to Adair, gave shelter to one of the evicted families; in March 1861 the local magistrates passed a resolution disassociating themselves from Adair and implying that he was the cause of his own troubles.

Whether conflict between 'new' landlords and their tenants was as common or inevitable as was thought, there was no doubt that Adair was a speculator in land. Between 1852 and his death in 1885, he was involved in over 70 major transactions in landed property—purchases, leases, sales, mortgages and redemptions. In the records of the Registry of Deeds in Dublin may be traced the history—complicated, tedious in its details, but dramatic in its consummation—of the formation of a great estate by the son of a small landed proprietor, between 1852 and 1885. Adair's achievements, whether measured in acres or wealth, were less than those of some of the better known 'new' landlords such as Allan Pollok in Galway; or, most remarkable of all, William Scully whose Irish estates were only part of his vast wealth, which by 1896 included over 200,000 acres in the U.S.A.[96] But in his own way, Adair was just as remarkable; starting with fewer resources than Pollok, and probably also than Scully, he built up an estate worth £140,000 by 1876, having added to a small family property worth about £20,000 by a complicated series of mortgages, purchases, and exchanges. Beginning in 1852, he spent £134,000 on purchases, raised £120,000 by mortgages and £112,000 by sales, and paid back £66,000 of the money raised by mortgage.[97]

The history of Adair's dealings in land falls into four stages: between 1852 and 1857 he bought almost 4,000 acres in County Tipperary, a townland of 600 acres in County Kilkenny, and the townlands of Ballinlough and Kilteale in the Queen's County; between 1857 and 1861, his energies were devoted almost exclusively to County Donegal; between 1861 and 1870, he bought nearly 9,000 acres in the Queen's County, including part of the duke of Leeds's estate at Graigue and land near his home at Bellegrove; after 1870 he consolidated his gains by selling his lands in Kildare and Kilkenny and exchanging the remainder of the Tipperary estate (part had been sold in the 1860s to pay for purchases) for more land in the Queen's County. Looking back from the vantage point of 1885, it is tempting to see a pattern in Adair's purchases: the purchase of scattered pieces of land in the 1850s when prices were low, later sold or exchanged for lands in his native county, culminating in the formation of a great estate where it could be most easily managed. But he may have originally intended to base himself in County Tipperary at Loughmoe, for some of his Tipperary purchases were close to each other; also, he assumed the grandiloquent address of 'Loughmore Castle', whose only basis in fact was the ruin, more correctly known as Loughmoe Castle.

The one remarkable diversion in the process of accumulation and consolidation was the purchases in County Donegal between 1857 and 1859: the lands bought were extensive but not valuable; they were not bargains by any standards; they were not sold to raise money for the purchase of land in the Queen's County; they were not obviously exploitable like the Tipperary lands. Also, apart from losses of rents between 1861 and 1868 when the Derryveagh lands were deserted, the building of Glenveagh Castle must have absorbed money that could have been more usefully employed in the late 1860s. If the grand design included the Donegal estate, romanticism must have tempered greed as a motive for acquiring it; it is understandable that someone who grew up in the dreary flat lands of north Queen's County and Kildare should be attracted by the wild mountain scenery of Donegal; it is less understandable that a land speculator who had already acquired valuable lands in the midlands should go so far north for lands that were poor. Not only did Donegal absorb and divert Adair's energies between 1857 and 1861 but also in 1863: that was the only year between 1852 and 1868 when he did not buy, sell, or mortgage land; it was also the year of Grierson's murder when Adair was reported by the police to be living with his 'confidential' housekeeper at Glenveagh.

Adair's ability to add purchase to purchase depended on his ability not only to mortgage the lands he bought but also to sell some of them profitably. The townlands of Ballinlough and Kilteale in the Queen's County are an example of purchase, mortgage, and resale following each other within a few years. Bought from the earl of Mornington in May 1855 by J. L. Maquay, a relation of Adair's, for £4,050, they were conveyed to Adair in February 1857; almost immediately he leased them to R. H. Farrar at an annual rent of £379. 12s. 6d.; on 4 July they were mortgaged for £4,100; two years later in 1859 the mortgage was redeemed, and they were again mortgaged, but for a larger sum; in 1860 they were again redeemed and sold early in 1861 for £7,960, a profit of almost 100 per cent.[98]

While there is no doubt that the basis of Adair's ability to raise money was advantageous sales and the vigorous exploitation of the mortgageable capacity of his purchases, he must also have had access to other funds. The table in the appendix below shows the flow of money from his first purchase in 1852 to his last mortgage in 1885: into his hands through sales and mortgages and out again through purchases and redemptions.[99] By 1875 money raised by sales and mortgages (£189,315) fell short of that disbursed on purchases and mortgages (£189,734) by £419; but the final column of the table, showing the balance between his incomings and outgoings, shows that it was not until 1876 that the balance was a credit one. In the first years of his career, 1852–3, he spent £18,740 without raising money by mortgage or sale; although the deficit fluctuated considerably, rising to £18,832 in 1858 and falling to £10,804 in 1865, Adair had access to credit of about £15,000 during his active career.

Adair and his father may have had savings; but their estate was small and the lavish farming operations of the father, while they do not exclude frugality, do not suggest it. In 1847 they had received £5,000 from William Steuart Trench for the townlands of Moher and Lackabrack;[100] this may have been the foundation of John George's career as a speculator, but it does not account for all of his resources. The balance may have been raised by creating equitable mortgages on the family estate by depositing its title deeds with a commercial bank or insurance company; such mortgages would not have been registered and their existence unnoted in the Registry of Deeds. It is possible, too, that Adair was able to raise money on his personal credit, or the personal credit of his relations; the earl of Gosford, for example, borrowed £59,430 from Coutts & Co. in the 1860s and 1870s merely on his personal credit and without the security of a registered mortgage.[101]

Another possibility is that Adair had partners; for example, in his purchases in Donegal and Kildare, he worked closely with a solicitor called John Anthony Hogan who was able to raise money for him.[102] Another partner may have been Samuel Frederick Adair, a Dublin solicitor, and historian and benefactor of the Rotunda Hospital, who handled much, but not all, of John George's legal business. There is evidence that he had funds to invest in mortgages;[103] although there is no evidence that he advanced money to John George on mortgage, he may, like many solicitors, have had funds that could be advanced for short periods on good security. Another possible partner was John George's wife, Cornelia, whom he married in 1867; in 1866, his deficit had shrunk, or been squeezed, to £10,804 but in 1867 it suddenly increased by £10,000 when he bought land in the Queen's County: he had to raise less than one third of the purchase price of £15,250 by a mortgage.[104] It is interesting that his wedding and honeymoon in 1867 did not prevent him from engaging in an elaborate series of transactions, even in the very month of his wedding; his inactivity in 1868, 1869, and 1870 may have been caused indirectly by his marriage: the valuation records suggest, for example, that renovations were made to Bellegrove in the late 1860s.

Although funds other than those raised by mortgages were important to Adair, mortgages were his main source of finance. Most of the purchases made in the early 1850s were mortgaged within a year or two; Loughmoe in County Tipperary, for example, bought on 26 June 1853, was mortgaged on 13 June 1854; Tinvoher, bought on 7 August 1852, was mortgaged also on 13 June 1854. Only one purchase made in the 1850s—Carrickloughmore and Curraghmore in Tipperary—remained unmortgaged for a relatively long time; bought on 15 November 1852, they were not mortgaged until 30 July 1859.[105] In the 1860s the speed with which lands were mortgaged was greater: Ballylehane, bought on 16 April 1861, was mortgaged within one month.[106] In 1864 the money to buy Rossmore was actually raised by an agreement to mortgage before the purchase was completed: the same device was used again in 1867.[107]

The identity of the mortgagees is interesting; they were not, for the most part, institutional lenders such as Scottish insurance companies or in trade (with one possible exception), but other landed gentry seeking secure investments for monies in their control. In the eighteen mortgage transactions between 1854 and 1885, the mortgagee in three was a relation of Adair through his maternal grandmother, John Leland Maquay, a banker 'now residing in the city of Florence'; in three, the mortgagees were Queen's County gentry such as the Hamilton Stubbers, or connected with them; in six they were members of landed families in other counties such as the Hon. Stephen Gough of Loughcooter Castle, County Galway, and James Saunderson of Castlesaunderson, County Cavan; in two the mortgagees were a clergyman in Derbyshire and a Miss Henrietta Sophia Greene of Union Lodge, Dungannon. Only in the remaining four transactions were the mortgagees institutions or in trade: in 1871 and 1872, two merchants and a doctor of medicine in Belfast advanced £15,000; in 1874, in two separate transactions, the Representative Church Body advanced £18,000.[108]

Apart from mortgagees who were relations or neighbours, it is possible to establish in one or two cases a personal connection between them and Adair. (Personal connections with the Queen's County mortgagees are easy to establish; Adair's father, for example, was a party to a Hamilton Stubber marriage settlement in 1848.[109]) A personal connection can also be established between Adair and one of the mortgagees who was not a Queen's County landlord: he was party to a family settlement with Henry Fitzgeorge Colley of Lucan Lodge, County Dublin, who lent him £5,030 in 1867.[110]

The largest mortgage transaction in which Adair was involved was a loan of £20,000 from Lord Digby in 1866, secured on the Donegal estate, which was hardly an adequate security for such a large sum. The Digby estate in the King's County was managed by Adair's uncle, William Steuart Trench, and his son, Thomas Weldon Trench. Their regime of management was almost as troubled as their kinsman's in County Donegal.[111] It would be misleading, however, to think that the Trenchs advanced Lord Digby's money to Adair on easy terms; the rate of interest charged was 6 per cent, the highest recorded in any of Adair's mortgages. But when the mortgage was executed, the financial world was disturbed by the Overend & Gurney crisis, and the bank rate stood at 10 per cent, the highest point it reached between 1822 and 1914; mortgagees usually expected a slightly higher rate of interest than the bank rate, so Adair did well to get a mortgage at 6 per cent during the worst financial crisis for years.

The £20,000 was used to purchase Roskeen in the Queen's County and was the largest sum ever given for a piece of land by Adair. It was not a bargain: its rents were low—less than £400 a year—and even if they were increased drastically, the return on capital would have been only 3 or 4 per cent. In the following year, 1867 (also the year of his marriage), he made his last major acquisition: 5,183 acres of the duke of Leeds's estate in the Queen's County.[112] In 1868 and 1869 he was involved in no registered transactions, and in the 1870s his momentum seems to have run down. The most dramatic transaction of the 1870s was not a purchase but an exchange: in 1875 he gave the remainder of his Tipperary estate to Sir John Craven Carden, Bt., of Templemore Abbey, County Tipperary, and received in exchange a smaller estate in the Queen's County and the sum of £2,536.[113] The 1870s had a conservative aspect: mortgages were redeemed, outlying lands were

Glenveagh Castle, County Donegal, c. 1900

sold, new mortgages reduced the difference between income and expenditure, and purchases were mainly confined to lands around Bellegrove. Symbolical of the loss of momentum, if not actually its cause, was the history of Roskeen, bought in 1866 with £20,000 borrowed from Lord Digby. Adair was not able to digest it and sold it to Lord Digby after three and a half years for £22,500.[114] Adair made an apparent profit of £2,500 since Digby released the lands mortgaged in 1866; but in fact he probably lost money in the transaction, for the mortgage had cost £4,400 in interest, less than half of which would have been recovered in rents from Roskeen.

The enigma of Adair's dealings in the 1870s, as suggested by the table in the appendix,[115] was that he raised money by mortgages and sales without buying much land. Ignoring the figures for 1875, which are an attempt to estimate the values of the lands exchanged with Sir John Craven Carden, he raised £73,555 by sales and mortgages, but spent just more than one third of this sum, £27,332, on purchases and redemptions. Not only was the notional deficit eliminated, but a credit balance of over £30,000 accrued by 1880. Why did he not put this money into land in the 1870s? There are several possible explanations: rising prices for land left fewer opportunities for picking up bargains;[116] the land act of 1870 inhibited evictions such as those at Derryveagh and made even the rearrangement of holdings difficult (according to Mrs Adair,'no intelligent American can understand the English government deliberately doing such an injustice to any class as that act did to the Irish landlords');[117] above all, a wave of rural disorder in 1869–70,[118] following the 'battle' of Ballycohey in 1868 and 'propagated by the contagion of the crime itself',[119] made aggressive estate management even more risky than it had been in 1859–63. It seems too that Adair's energies were diverted into other channels through his marriage in 1867 to Cornelia Ritchie.

When Mrs Adair died in 1921, her will included bequests of over $1,000,000 as well as the Donegal and Queen's County estates; there were references to a ranch in Texas and landed property in New York; in the United Kingdom, as well as the Irish estates, there were references to an estate at Ashwell Rise in Rutland and to houses in Oakley Street, Chelsea.[120] Apart from the fact that a will is not necessarily an accurate inventory of assets, it is not easy to be certain about the relationship between her property and Adair's. By 1921 much of the tenanted land on the Queen's County estate had been sold under the land purchase acts at good prices—about eighteen years' purchase—but this money, even if converted into American property, could not have accounted for more than a fraction of her estate; by 1914 sales totalling just over £42,000 had been made, but converted into American dollars this was less than one fifth of Mrs Adair's estate in 1921.[121] Even when the sums raised by sales and mortgages in the 1870s are added to the money received under the land purchase acts, they could not account for an estate of more than $1,000,000.

It seems that some at least of Mrs Adair's property in America was created by her husband's speculations in the U.S.A. in the 1870s: he visited the U.S.A. frequently, in 1874 and in 1876, for example, when he met Colonel Charles Goodnight ('a trail blazer and Indian scout') in Denver. Adair and Goodnight went into partnership and acquired land in the Palo Duro canyon in Texas, where they established the JA ranch, consisting of 500,000 acres, 30,000 cattle and 700 horses.[122] Certainly, Adair's property seems to have been great when he made his will in 1883: he left all his property to his wife, but he made complicated provisions for the disposal of his American property if she died before him. Among these were legacies of £43,000 to be paid out of his American property before it was divided equally between Mrs Adair's two sons by her first marriage and William Disney Maquay.[123] This, of course, proves nothing conclusively about the size of Adair's American wealth, but it does suggest that it was considerably in excess of £40,000 and may well have been as great as his Irish estate. The fact remains, however, that unless Adair was very successful in the 1870s, his wife must either have been rich when he married her in 1867, or acquired great wealth after Adair's death in 1885. Whether his marriage in 1867 brought him a wealthy wife, or drew his attention to investment outside Ireland and accounted for the slowing down of his activities here, or whether matrimony dulled the edge of acquisitive appetite, is unclear; but the discrepancy between Mrs Adair's estate in 1921 and what she would have had as the widow of an Irish landlord was great. When Adair signed the marriage register on 29 May 1867, he may have secured an investment that was more lucrative than anything to be had in the Landed Estates Court.

Apart from any possibility of wider activities, Adair's success as a land speculator in Ireland was remarkable. An idea of his success can be gained merely by looking at some of his sales and exchanges: Knavinstown in County Kildare, bought on lease in 1861 for £5,235 and the freehold purchased for £1,032 in 1874, was sold for £15,830 in 1876; part of the Tipperary estate, bought in the early 1850s for £17,475, was exchanged in 1875 for the equivalent of £36,700; the remainder was bought for £7,574 and sold for £13,000.

It is possible to calculate roughly the value of Adair's landed property in 1876 by assuming a certain rate of purchase and a known burden of mortgages. For all its uncertainty, this demonstrates Adair's success: in 1876 the Donegal, Queen's County, and other estates were worth £142,000; outstanding morgages totalled £43,330, but there was a cash balance of £20,411; in other words, Adair was worth about £120,000. This does not include any allowance for improvements such as the house at Glenveagh, or the gardens at Bellegrove; nor is it based on the assumption that Adair's lands were more highly rented than average, although there is considerable evidence to show that this was

Rathdaire (formerly Bellegrove), County Leix, 1982.

the case. If it is assumed that Adair's paternal estate was worth about £18,000, he had increased his wealth six-fold by successful speculation between 1852 and 1876.[124] In addition he had extended the house at Bellegrove, beautified its demesne by the construction of an ornamental lake, built Glenveagh Castle, and paid off, or recovered, much of the money he had borrowed by means other than registered mortgages. To this process of accumulation, the Donegal estate contributed little; in the calculation above it was assumed to be worth £20,000 but it had cost Adair at least £16,000.[125] Compared with lands purchased in Kildare, Kilkenny and Tipperary, this was a poor rate of appreciation; it had also distracted his attention for nearly four years at a time when there were still bargains to be had. Although there is much that is false in Adair's claims about his actions in County Donegal, it is difficult to resist the conclusion that he had indeed been 'enchanted by the surpassing beauty of the scenery'.

10 The management of Adair's estates

If the Derryveagh evictions were all that was known about Adair's speculations, it would be an easy matter to fit him into the contemporary picture of the land shark who enhanced the value of his purchases by the wholesale eviction of the small, unprofitable tenants on his estate and replaced them with big farmers who could pay high rents. The interesting, and puzzling, aspect of Adair's estate management was that it did not conform completely to this pattern. It is possible to examine the movement of tenants on the other parts of his estates by means of the manuscript records of the tenement valuation. The result shows that, with some exceptions, there were no sweeping changes of tenants. The exceptions were Ballinlough and Kilteale in the Queen's County, bought in 1857 and sold in 1861 at a great profit; Knavinstown in County Kildare, bought in 1861 and sold in 1876; and possibly, Tinvoher in County Tipperary, purchased in 1852 and exchanged in 1876.[126]

The first of these, Ballinlough and Kilteale, are a good example of what could be done with land in the 1850s. When bought by Adair, there were four tenants, one of whom was quite substantial, occupying half of the area of the two townlands; almost immediately they were replaced by one tenant, T. H. Farrar, who was given a lease for ever, at a rent subject to periodic increases.[127] The new rent, even at its starting point, was more than twice the old rent; even by Irish standards, the old rents were low; by the same standards, the new rents were very high. The same drastic system was applied to Knavinstown in 1865; four years after its purchase, most of it was leased to two farmers in partnership, replacing several fairly large tenants, at a rent more than twice the tenement valuation of the whole townland.[128] (The tenement valuation, carried out under the supervision of Sir Richard Griffith in the 1850s and 1860s, was a rough guide to the letting value of land; on most Irish estates rents were about 20 or 30 per cent above it.)

In the third case where evictions seem to have been common—the Tipperary lands bought in 1852 and 1853—the process was more a drastic reduction of the number of tenants than the sweeping away of all of them. It seems to have been in Tinvoher and Curraghmore in Tipperary, near the village of Loughmoe, that the fifteen evictions returned by the police took place in the second quarter of 1853.[129] A comparison of the valuation books with the incumbered estates court rentals shows the disappearance of several small tenants and the appearance, in the place of some of them, of Adam Grierson, Adair's steward in Donegal, with 123 acres valued at over £100, a very substantial holding of good land.[130] But the two townlands were not completely depopulated like Derryveagh: the census of 1851 recorded 71 houses in the two townlands; in 1861 the number had fallen to 42; in 1881 it was 34.

There is no evidence of drastic changes on the remaining lands purchased; in 1861, for example, it was alleged that Adair had served notices to quit on 27 of the 33 tenants of Ballylehane, bought in the Landed Estates Court in April 1861; but the valuation records show that these were not enforced. Even in the case of Roskeen, bought at a fancy price in 1867, where the obvious strategy would have been the rapid eviction of all the tenants and their replacement by one or two big tenants, the sitting tenants were left undisturbed.

While the clearing away of small tenants was a part of Adair's strategy, it was not his most frequently used weapon. (It was, of course, an effective weapon as the profitable sales of Ballinlough and Kilteale and Knavinstown showed.) Like many other Irish landlords, Adair found that small tenants were often as useful as large ones, when it came to paying rents; he seems, in fact, to have been satisfied in many cases with simply increasing the rents of the tenants he found on the lands he bought. In the absence of estate papers and rentals, there is no explicit evidence of what Adair was trying to do; but the records of the Irish Land Commission show that he increased many of his rents drastically. In the first ten years after the passing of the land act of 1881, the land courts reduced nearly half of the rents in the country; the reduced rents were about 30 per cent above the tenement valuation and were reduced by 21 per cent. During the same period, about half of Adair's rents on the Queen's County estate were reduced; they had been about 55 per cent above the valuation and were reduced by 27 per cent. On the Donegal estate about half of the rents were reduced by 27 per cent from 33 per cent above the valuation. Compared with Ireland as a whole, the rents on Adair's estates, especially the Queen's County estate, were relatively high; on one part of the Queen's County estate, for example, bought in 1867, almost half of the rents seem to have been increased by 50 per cent in the 1870s.

The weakness of the returns of judicial rents fixed by the land courts, as a source of information on rents as they were before 1881, is their silence on those that did not come before the courts. The records of sales under the land purchase acts of 1891 and 1903, however, give the rents of holdings sold, whether the rents were fixed by the courts or not. These show that one third of the rents on Adair's Queen's County estate were actually low—about equal to the tenement valuation. Whether this represents the state of these rents before 1881, or reflects reductions made by Adair, or Mrs Adair perhaps, after 1881, under pressure during the land war, is not clear. But it is worth noting that they were lower than the judicial rents, which even after an average reduction of 27 per cent were 14 per cent above the valuation.

It is tempting to place Adair at the extremes of possible landlord behaviour. Compared with most Irish landlords he was vigorous and ruthless: he bought and sold and with a frequency unusual in established landed families; he increased his rents by larger amounts than was usual;[131] he brought a doctrinaire fussiness to his dealings with tenants, where most landlords were content to swim with the tide; above all, he was involved in one of the most controversial incidents in the history of the land question between the famine and the land war. Not only is it tempting to place Adair at the extreme limits of landlord behaviour, but to place him at the extremes of ordinary, respectable Victorian behaviour: two of his servants had been murdered, he had a doubtful reputation for accuracy, he was the subject of a debate in parliament, he carried on a disreputable liaison with a servant, and became the subject of a scurrilous novel and two ballads. Few Irish landlords were so visible.

11 Conclusion

Finally what became of the main actors in the Derryveagh drama? The fate of the evicted tenants was varied, but almost generally harsh. Of the 9 families allowed to remain in their holdings after giving up possession to the sub-sheriff, only 3 were permanently reinstated; the rest were gradually removed in the months after April 1861. Of the families turned out in April, 5 were fortunate enough to find work on neighbouring estates or to have small patches of land not on the Adair estate; 13 families went to the workhouse in Letterkenny; of the remaining 20, 6 found shelter with friends but 14 were either unaccounted for or still wandering through the ruins of the cottages a month later. For some it was the end: old John Doherty of Castletown died in the workhouse after admission; Michael Bradley went mad and after trying to drown himself, was committed; for others eviction was the beginning of a new life in Australia.

An appeal was launched by the catholic bishop of Raphoe, assisted by Henry Maturin the rector of Gartan, the priest Daniel Kair, and the presbyterian minister Sampson Jack; the Donegal Celtic Relief Committee was formed in Melbourne and the assistance of distinguished Irishmen in Australia, such as Charles Gavan Duffy, was secured; and plans were made to pay the passages of the younger members of the evicted families who wanted to emigrate. On 18 January 1862 Inspector Armstrong of the D.M.P. reported that '143 young men and women, emigrants for Australia, arrived by train at 6 p.m. ... on their way from Derryveagh, County Donegal. They proceeded along Talbot Street, Henry Street, and Mary Street, to Mr Fleming's hotel where they got refreshments; after a while they proceeded to the North Wall, accompanied by a clergyman, where they embarked between 8 and 9 o'clock p.m., together with 130 young men and women from Gweedore, County Donegal, on board the *Lady Eglinton*, steamer for Melbourne, *via* Plymouth. They were all conducted on board by a Roman Catholic clergyman. All passed off quietly and in good order'. After the dinner in Fleming's hotel Father McFadden, who seems to have been the clergyman mentioned above, addressed the emigrants in Gaelic, urging them not to neglect their religious duties, to say their night and morning prayers, to approach the Blessed Eucharist at Christmas and Easter, to write to the old people at home and not to forget 'poor old Ireland'. (This last injunction was received 'with intense emotion and cries of "Never—never, God knows!"')[132]

The fates of the other participants were also varied. Adam Grierson, who had supervised the evictions, was murdered in April 1863, having been dismissed by Adair and being on the point of emigrating to Queensland. What became of Mrs Murray and the shepherds, Rankin and Campbell, is not clear; but they were not brought to justice, and Rankin and Mrs Murray did not set up house on the Adair estate.[133] The only person to be punished severely by the law for his misdeeds in 1861 was the informer, William Deery, who was sentenced to seven years penal servitude by Mr Justice Ball at the assizes in March 1861. In October 1863 he appealed to the lord lieutenant for remission of his sentence, pleading that 'previous to his great calamity (which he has ever since deplored and deeply repented of) [he] always had the character of an honest and industrious man supporting a young and helpless family by honest labour'.[134] His plea for mercy was rejected: the trial judge reported that 'the sentence was the heaviest I was empowered by the law to award, and I am not aware of any mitigating circumstances whatever'; the police, also consulted, reported that Deery's character before his conviction was 'exceedingly bad'.

Adair, the chief actor in the drama, continued his career of land speculation with apparently unabated vigour until the late 1860s. He achieved those pinnacles of local greatness that he seems to have coveted, serving the office of sheriff in the Queen's County 1867-8, and in County Donegal 1873-4; he also became a deputy lieutenant of both counties. But some disapproval of neighbours or county authorities still persisted, for he was not the first choice for the shrievalty in either case: in Donegal he was placed second on the judges' list to James B. Delap, who declined service because his wife's confinement was 'to take place in London (for the first time) as nearly as possible at the exact period when the spring assizes are usually held in my county'. Delap suggested as his replacement, not Adair, but John Stouppe Charley of Aranmore, who was third on the list.[135] In the Queen's County, he was appointed only after two judges' lists of six names had failed to produce a sheriff.[136] It was also significant that he did not become a magistrate in the Queen's County until 1867, the year he served the office of sheriff, and the year of his marriage.

His wife, Cornelia Ritchie, was the daughter of a general and the widow of a colonel in the U.S. army. Mrs Adair was considerably younger than her second husband: she was 31 and he 44 at the time of their marriage. The house at Glenveagh seems to have been completed in the early 1870s (work had been delayed by a fire—not, it seems, a malicious one), and they entertained there in the 1870s and 1880s: Emily Lawless was a guest in 1878.[137] Mrs Adair seems to have enjoyed the life of an Irish chatelaine: she fenced the deer park at Glenveagh in 1891 and introduced red deer from Perthshire and Caithness in 1891 and 1892, and from Fermanagh and Lincolnshire in 1909 and 1910 (the pattern of deer displacing the sheep that had earlier driven out the human population was a well established one in Scotland);[138] she also extended Glenveagh Castle after her husband's death and when Rathdaire was burnt she moved into a house on the demesne (the census returns of both 1901 and 1911 show that she maintained establishments in both Donegal and the Queen's County).[139] The Adairs, especially Mrs Adair, were well established figures in late Victorian society: Mrs Adair's sister, Elizabeth Post, married the future Lord Barrymore, an alliance with a family that was as well known as Adair's in the troubled history of the Irish land question; a photograph taken at Glenveagh in 1902 shows Mrs Adair at the height of her hospitable glory, with a stalking party that included the duke and duchess of Connaught, Princess Margaret of Connaught, the duchess of Abercorn and John and Leone Leslie.[140]

Adair died in St Louis, Missouri, in 1885, aged 62; his wife died in London in 1921. They had no children, and by a will made in 1883 all his property passed to Mrs Adair in absolute ownership. If Mrs Adair had died before her husband, most of his property would have gone to William Disney Maquay of Florence, a banker and related to Adair through his paternal grandmother. (Some of his property would also have gone to Mrs Adair's two sons by her first marraige and to her sister, Mrs Post.) One provision of the will, however, was typical of Adair's obsession with territorial aggrandizement: Maquay was to 'assume and use under licence from the Crown or otherwise the surname of Adair in addition to his own present surname (but so that the name of Adair shall be the last and principal name)'.[141]

The dispersal of the lands accumulated by Adair began soon after his death: the first sales of the Queen's County estate took place under the land act of 1891 and by 1914 half of the estate was sold. After the establishment of the Irish Free State the remaining tenanted land was sold and the demesne at Bellegrove was broken up. Although the tenanted land on the Donegal estate was sold, a great area of the estate, including the lands cleared in 1861, remained intact and

Rathdaire church 1982. Built in 1887 by Cornelia Adair in memory of her husband and his father.

connected to Glenveagh Castle. After Mrs Adair's death in 1921, the remnants of the Donegal estate passed to her grandson (by her first marriage), Montgomery Wadsworth Ritchie, and then to Arthur Kingsley Porter of Cambridge, Mass., who was drowned in July 1933. In 1938 it was purchased by Mr Henry McIlhenny, also an American, who planned and executed the gardens—'now one of the great gardens of the British Isles'.[142] By one of those ironies, not unusual in Irish history, the house and lands of Glenveagh, including the Derryveagh estate, have passed from Mr McIlhenny to the Forest and Wildlife Service, and plans are in progress to turn the estate into a national park: one of the few pieces of the land of Ireland to pass into the ownership of the people of Ireland does so because of a great act of landlord tyranny in 1861.

There is a tradition in County Donegal, almost too appropriate to be true, that Adair took precautions to provide himself with a monument; a sculptor from 'far away' was employed and the inscription 'John Adair, just, generous and true' was chiselled on a boulder above Lough Veagh; a few nights after the work was completed it was struck by lightning and the fragments hurled into the lake below.[143] After his death, Mrs Adair took great pains to erect a memorial to him: a hospital at Clarendon in Texas was named 'Adair Hospital' and in her will she left it $35,000; at Ballyadding, between Ballybrittas and Bellegrove, she built a church in 1887 to the memory of her husband and his father; in her will she left $20,000 to the R.C.B. to erect a new parish, to be called 'Rathdaire', out of the parish of Lea, with her church as its centre.

After his death in St Louis, Adair's body was brought back to Ireland for burial in the churchyard at Lea, near Ballybrittas. A plain stone was placed over the grave with the simple inscription: 'John George Adair, born 3 March 1823, died 14 May 1885'. Much of Adair's life had been spent in the company of Americans; in death, he has the company of an American author, the sub-title of whose best-known book, might serve as an epitaph: within yards of Adair's last piece of Irish landed property is buried Edward Shepherd Mead, author of *How to succeed in business without really trying. The dastard's guide to fame and fortune.*

References

1. Information about the evictions and the events that preceded them is taken from two complementary sources: S.P.O., R.P. 1861/7273, and letters, memoranda and newscuttings concerning the state of Donegal, compiled by Sir Thomas Larcom 1856-66 (N.L.I., MS 7633). (The latter is hereafter cited as Larcom papers, Donegal.)
2. *Hansard 3*, clxii, 523, 842, 847; clxiii, 470, 1487-1514; clxiv, 113, 243-52.
3. Copies 'of all requisitions, reports, notices and correspondence from or to the sheriff or sub-sheriff of the county of Donegal etc.', H.C. 1861 (249), lii, 559; Copies 'of any correspondence that has taken place between J. G. Adair, Esq., and the Irish government, on the subject of extra police in the county of Donegal, and of certain evictions that have taken place in that county', H.C. 1861 (274), lii, 579.
4. *F.J.*, 13 Apr. 1861, *L.S.*, 11 Apr. 1861, and *The Nation*, 13 Apr. 1861; these and other newscuttings are to be found in Larcom papers, Donegal.
5. *Glenveigh, or the victims of vengeance: a tale of Irish peasant life in the present* (Boston, 1870). One of the ballads, by the eccentric fenian, Thomas Neilson Underwood, was published in the preface of Cassidy's novel; the other, 'The lovers of Glenveagh', may be found in Larcom papers, Donegal.
6. *I.L.N.*, 13 & 20 Apr. 1861.
7. S.P.O., R.P. 1861/7273.
8. A. M. Sullivan, *New Ireland* (London, 1877), i, 252.
9. William Allingham, *Laurence Bloomfield in Ireland; or the new landlord* (London, 1869), p. 142.
10. Patrick Lavelle, *The Irish landlord since the revolution* (Dublin, 1870), p. 272.
11. See for example the official tourist guide of the Great Northern (Ireland) Railway.
12. Stephen Gwynn, *Highways and byways in Donegal and Antrim* (London, 1899), pp 89-92.
13. Dominic Ó Ceallaigh, 'Glenveagh' in *Donegal Annual*, vi, no. 2 (1965), pp 150-60.
14. Alastair Rowan, *The buildings of Ireland: North west Ulster* (London, 1979), pp 309-10.
15. Liam Dolan, *Land war and eviction in Derryveagh 1840-65* (Dundalk, 1980).
16. John Cornforth, 'Glenveagh Castle, County Donegal. The home of Mr

Henry P. McIlhenny' in *Country Life*, 3 & 10 June 1982, pp 1636–40, 1734–7.

17. Registry of Deeds, Dublin, 1859/42/136.
18. Bateman, *Great Landowners*; Reg. Deeds 1857/25/91; ibid., 36/231; 1858/13/128; 14/16; 1859/43/155.
19. There was officially no such place in Queen's County as Rathdaire but both Adair and his father used this as their address from 1871. *Thom's Directory* shows that they experimented a little before settling on Rathdaire: in 1865 their address was Bellegrove; in 1866–8, 'Ballafabole'; in 1869–70, Bellegrove.
20. *Irish Farmers' Gazette*, 18 Feb. 1865.
21. P.R.O.I., incumbered estates commrs, index of conveyances, ii, 3095 & 3154 (7 Aug. 1852); ibid., iii, 3414 & 3914 (26 Jan. & 4 June 1853); v, 6193 (18 July 1855); vi, 6599, 6984 & 7257 (23 May, 19 July & 30 July 1856); Reg. Deeds, 1852/26/109–10; 1857/5/51.
22. *Irish Farmers' Gazette*, 29 Apr. 1855.
23. Cassidy, *Glenveigh*, p. 25.
24. Marquis of Lansdowne, *Glanerought and the Petty-Fitzmaurices* (London, 1937), p. 141.
25. Rowan, *North west Ulster*, p. 310.
26. James Godkin, *The land-war in Ireland* (London, 1870), p. 391.
27. Lansdowne, *Glanerought*, p. 138.
28. William Steuart Trench, *Realities of Irish life* (London, 1868).
29. *Irish Farmers' Gazette*, 10 Apr. 1858.
30. Larcom papers (N.L.I., MS 7639, no. 95).
31. Ibid., no. 104; see below, p. 55.
32. Ibid., no. 86.
33. Ibid., no. 122.
34. Ibid., no. 97.
35. *A return 'of the outrages specially reported by the constabulary as committed within the barony of Kilmacrenan, County Donegal, during the last ten years'*, H.C. 1861 (404), lii, 585.
36. *Report from the select committee on destitution (Gweedore and Cloughaneely); together with the proceedings of the committee, minutes of evidence, appendix and index*, H.C. 1857–8 (412), 89.
37. *The Evening Packet*, 28 Oct., 1858, *The Daily Express*, 19 Nov. 1860, *Northern Whig*, 12 Apr. 1861; these and other newcuttings are to be found in Larcom papers, Donegal.
38. Patrick Lavelle, *The war in Partry; or, proselytism and eviction on the part of Bishop Plunket of Tuam* (Dublin, 1861); *Partry and Glenveagh: a letter to the Rt Hon. E. W. Cardwell, M.P., chief secretary for Ireland* (Dublin, 1861); see also S.P.O., R.P. 1861/7272.
39. *Hansard 3*, clxiv, 413–36.
40. See the ballad by Underwood in Cassidy, *Glenveigh*, pp iv–v.
41. *An act for the protection and relief of the destitute poor evicted from their dwellings in Ireland*, 11 & 12 Vic. c. 47 (10 Aug. 1848).

42. S.P.O., *Irish crimes records, 1848–93.*
43. Robert Curtis, *The history of the Royal Irish Constabulary* (2nd ed., Dublin & London, 1871), p. 105.
44. Ibid., pp 103–4.
45. Sir Henry Brownrigg, *Examination of some recent allegations concerning the constabulary force in Ireland, in a report to his excellency the lord lieutenant* (Dublin, 1864), p. 21.
46. *Remarks on Ireland; as it is; as it ought to be; and as it might be...* (London, 1849), pp 29–30.
47. Larcom papers, Donegal.
48. S.P.O., R.P. 1874/685 and *Return 'by provinces and counties (compiled from returns made to the inspector-general, Royal Irish Constabulary) of cases of evictions which have come to the knowledge of the constabulary in each of the years from 1849 to 1880, inclusive',* H.C. 1881 (185), lxxvii, 725. For summaries of evictions and agrarian outrages, see T. W. Moody, *Davitt and Irish revolution 1846–82* (Oxford, 1982), pp 562–3, 565–6.
49. See Galway 1855, Kerry 1859, Mayo 1858, and Westmeath 1857.
50. Godkin, *The land-war in Ireland,* p. 391; Trench, *Realities,* pp 311–31.
51. S.P.O., official papers, 1851, no. 28: return of evictions for the quarters ending 30 June, 30 Sept, and 31 Dec.
52. *Judicial statistics, Ireland, 1863* [3418], H.C. 1864, lvii, 653; see also *Miscellaneous statistics of the United Kingdom, pt V,* [3398], H.C. 1864, lix, 1; *pt VI,* [3722], H.C. 1866, lxxiv, 443; *pt VII,* [4158], H.C. 1868–9, lxii, 127.
53. Brownrigg, *Examination,* pp 58, 63.
54. See occupations in *Census Ire., 1861.*
55. *Misc. statistics, U.K., pt VII,* p. 64 [4158], H.C. 1868–9, lxii, 198; *Statistical tables relating to colonial and other possessions, pt XIII* [4194–1], H.C. 1868–9, lxiii, 131.
56. See, for example, Emile Zola, *Earth* (trans. by Ann Linday, Arrow Books, 1967).
57. Trench, *Realities,* pp 197–8.
58. S.P.O., R.P. 1862/19,409.
59. Ibid., 1861/9434.
60. Ibid., 1862/10,395.
61. Ibid., Crime dept., 'B' files, carton 1, B 134.
62. Ibid., R.P. 1862/10,395.
63. Ibid., 1869/5522.
64. Ibid., *Irish crimes records, 1848–93.*
65. Theobald Dillon, R.M. to Sir Thomas Larcom, 30 May 1861 in Larcom papers, Donegal; the letter is reproduced in Dolan, *Land war in Derryveagh,* pp 181–90.
66. *A return 'of the outrages specially reported by the constabulary as committed within the barony of Kilmacrenan, County Donegal, during the last ten years',* H.C. 1861 (404), lii, 585.

67. Cassidy, *Glenveigh*, pp iii, 46–7, 53–4, 147–55, 203.
68. *Hansard 3*, clxiii, 1508.
69. Ibid., clxiv, 251.
70. Sullivan, *New Ireland*, ii, 350–71.
71. Ibid., ii, 364, 369.
72. Cassidy, *Glenveigh*, p. 29.
73. Leon Ó Broin, *Fenian fever. An Anglo-American dilemma* (London, 1971), p. 112.
74. *Report from the select committee on the Tenure and Improvement of Land (Ireland) Act; together with the proceedings of the committee etc.*, H.C. 1865 (402), xi, 341; *Report from the select committee of the house of lords on the Tenure (Ireland) Bill* [*H.L.*]; *together with the proceedings of the committee etc.*, H.C. 1867 (518), xiv, 423.
75. J. H. Whyte, *The independent Irish party, 1850–9* (Oxford, 1958), *passim*; Walker, *Irish parliamentary results*, pp 94–98.
76. Whyte, op. cit., p. 150.
77. S.P.O., R.P. 1853/11, 351.
78. *Hansard 3*, clxiii, 1504.
79. For an account of William Scully and his family, see Homer F. Socolofsky, *Landlord William Scully* (Kansas, 1979).
80. S.P.O., R.P. 1850/1/6482.
81. Ibid., 1862/20, 122.
82. Valuation Office, Dublin: cancelled books for County Donegal/Letter-kenny/Gartan.
83. *Report from the select committee on general valuation (Ireland); together with the proceedings of the committee etc.*, p. 61, H.C. 1868–9 (362), ix, 73.
84. The papers relating to this case are not available in the S.P.O., but the indexes and registers give a rough idea of the course of events; see S.P.O., R.P. 1869/14, 846 and 1873/6130.
85. Department of Irish Folklore, University College, Dublin: S 1072, p. 355.
86. I am indebted to Dr R. V. Comerford of St Patrick's College, Maynooth, for information on the spread of fenianism. See S.P.O., fenian papers, abstracts of cases, ii, 607 for Underwood; see also S.P.O., list of warrants under the *habeas corpus* suspension act, 1866 and index of names, 1862–5.
87. Ibid., Irish land league and Irish national league papers, cartons 1–4.
88. *Freeman's Journal*, 21 Jan. 1881. (I am indebted to Dr Moody for this reference.)
89. James McFadden, *The present and the past of the agrarian struggle in Gweedore: with letters on railway extension* (Londonderry, 1889).
90. H. W. Massingham, *The Gweedore hunt. A story of English justice in Ireland* (London, 1889), p. 6.
91. *Report of the evicted tenants commission*, ii; *minutes of evidence, appendices and index*, pp 132, 465 [C 6935-I], H.C. 1893–4, xxxi.
92. James Hack Tuke, *Irish distress and its remedies. The land question. A*

visit to Donegal and Connaught in the spring of 1880 (4th ed., London, 1880), p. 84.

93. S.P.O., Irish crimes records, 1881, lists of warrants and arrests under the Protection of Person and Property (Ireland) Act, 1881.

94. Ibid., Irish land league and Irish national league papers, carton 10.

95. Ibid., Crime dept., B files, carton 1, B 134.

96. Socolofsky, *Landlord William Scully*, p. 126.

97. See below, pp 77–8.

98. P.R.O.I., incumbered estates commrs, index of conveyances, v, 5810; Reg. Deeds, 1857/5/51, 171–2; ibid., 1859/28/267–8; 1860/34/276; 1861/2/58.

99. See below, pp 77–8.

100. Reg. Deeds, 1847/25/240, 250; ibid., 1855/9/223.

101. Letters of William Wann to Lord Gosford, 1875–8 (P.R.O.N.I., D 1606/5A/4, p. 76).

102. Reg. Deeds, 1860/11/51.

103. See for example Reg. Deeds, 1870/31/123.

104. See below, p. 77.

105. P.R.O.I., incumbered estates commrs, index of conveyances, ii, 3095; iii, 3414; Reg. Deeds, 1852/26/109; ibid., 1854/15/16; 1859/28/268.

106. Reg. Deeds, 1861/16/209.

107. Ibid., 1864/22/95; 29/30; 1867/13/246; 30/149.

108. Ibid., 1854/15/16; 1855/8/169; 1856/10/70; 1857/19/156; 1858/1/124; 1859/28/268–9; 1861/16/209; 1864/22/95; 1866/21/206; 1867/13/246; 1871/28/255; 1872/12/161; 1874/14/198; 33/64; 1876/2/160; 1878/16/85; 1885/10/135.

109. Ibid., 1848/5/26.

110. Ibid., 1867/13/246; 1871/1/122.

111. See above p. 19.

112. Reg. Deeds, 1867/23/130.

113. Ibid., 1875/19/190; 20/260.

114. Ibid., 1866/36/126; 1867/1/164; 1870/10/281.

115. See below, pp 77–8.

116. W. N. Hancock, *Report on the state of Ireland in 1874* (Dublin, 1874), p. 38.

117. Cornelia Adair, *My diary, August 30 to November 5, 1874* (repr., University of Texas Press, 1965), p. 125.

118. S.P.O., Irish crimes records, 1869–70.

119. *Hansard 3*, cc, 92.

120. P.R.O.I., wills & admons, 1922.

121. This information is taken from the returns of sales under the land purchase acts, published in the parliamentary papers; full references may be found in *General alphabetical index to the bills, reports, etc. ... 1890–99*, H.C. 1904 (368), cxii; *General index to the bills, reports, etc. ... 1900 to 1948–9* (London, 1960).

122. For Adair's American ventures, see Mrs Adair, *My diary*, Harley True Burton *A history of the JA ranch* (Austin, 1928) and W. G. Kerr, *Scottish capital on the American credit frontier* (Austin, 1976). (I am indebted to John Cornforth for giving me copies of the relevant passages of Burton and Kerr, which demonstrate not only the extent of Adair's involvement in America, but the shrewdness of his dealings.)

123. Copy of the last will and testament of J. G. Adair (Irish Land Comm., Record Dept., box 3236 (sch. B, no. 17, record no. E.C. 6320).

124. Details of the extent and value of the estates are to be found in the registered deeds, Bateman's *Great landowners* and a map of Adair's estates in the Queen's County (N.L.I., 16 M 20).

125. The value of the Donegal estate in 1876 was calculated by assuming that its rental was 20 per cent above the tenement valuation and that it would have sold for 22 years' purchase. The price paid for two parts of the estate in 1850s was not specified in the deeds; two other parts were bought for £2,400 and £8,000; Derryveagh was acquired by a fee farm grant at an annual rent of £225, the equivalent of a capital outlay of £4,500. See Reg. Deeds, 1857/25/91; 36/231; 1858/13/128; 14/16, 231; 1859/42/136, 43/155.

126. Valuation Office, Dublin: cancelled books for the Queen's County/Carlow/Ballylehane; ibid., Mountmellick/Ballybrittas, Ballyfin, Cappalough, Garrymore, Graigue, Jamestown, Kilcolmanbane and Sallyford; Slievemargy/Rossmore; County Kildare/Lackagh/Athy; County Kilkenny/Urlingford/Athy; County Tipperary/Carrick-on-Suir/Garrangibbon; Loughmoe East/Thurles.

127. P.R.O.I., incumbered estates court rentals, xxiv, earl of Mornington's estate; Reg. Deeds, 1857/5/171-2.

128. Ibid., 1865/11/93.

129. S.P.O., R.P. 1853/11, 351. See above, p. 45.

130. P.R.O.I., incumbered estates court rentals, xiv, estate of Sir George Goold.

131. W. E. Vaughan, 'An assessment of the economic performance of Irish landlords, 1851–81' in F. S. L. Lyons and R. A. J. Hawkins (ed.), *Ireland under the union: Varieties of tension: Essays in honour of T. W. Moody* (Oxford, 1980).

132. Sullivan, *New Ireland*, ii, 71–5.

133. S.P.O.., convict reference books, 1860–66.

134. Ibid., convict petitions 1863, 'D'.

135. Ibid., official papers, 1873, no. 16.

136. Ibid., 1867, no. 3.

137. I am indebted to Mr Henry P. McIlhenny, Glenveagh Castle, County Donegal for this information from a visitors' book in his possession.

138. John Cornforth, 'Glenveagh Castle, County Donegal. The home of Mr Henry P. McIlhenny' in *Country Life*, 10 June 1982, p. 1736.

139. P.R.O.I., Census Ire., 1901 & 1911, enumerators' forms, County Donegal, no. 88, Mullangore; ibid., the Queen's County, no. 68, Bellegrove.

140. Anita Leslie, *Edwardians in love* (London, 1974), pp 336–7; for a reference to Mrs Adair and 'Princess May and the Tecks' see also Anita Leslie, *Mr Frewen of England. A Victorian adventurer* (London, 1966).
141. For Adair's will, see above note 123; for the many ramifications of Adair's family, see T. R. F. Cooke-Trench, *A memoir of the Trench family* (privately printed, 1897).
142. Mark Bence-Jones, *Burke's guide to country houses*, i, *Ireland* (London, 1978), p. 139.
143. Dominic Ó Ceallaigh, 'Glenveagh' in *Donegal Annual*, vi, no. 2 (1965), p. 157.

Appendix

Adair's transactions in landed property in Ireland, 1852–85

The following table gives the amount of *capital* raised annually by sales and mortgages, and spent on purchases of land and the redemption of mortgages. (The table does not attempt to measure Adair's *income* from sources other than borrowing, e.g. from rents of the estates he had bought.)

The purchases recorded here for 1857 do not include two in County Donegal for which no purchase prices were given in the deeds; the figure of £5,000 for purchases in 1859 is an estimate, as is the figure for sales in 1875.

year	no. of transactions	income (£s) mortgages	sales	expenditure (£s) purchases	redemptions	balance (£s)
1852	2	—	—	7,215	—	—7,215
1853	2	—	—	11,525	—	—18,740
1854	2	7,400	1,543	—	—	—9,797
1855	2	3,000	—	5,260	—	—12,057
1856	5	4,000	—	7,575	—	—15,632
1857	7	4,100	2,150	4,050	—	—13,432
1858	3	5,000	—	10,400	—	—18,832
1859	4	6,000	—	5,000	1,000	—18,832
1860	1	—	—	—	—	—18,832
1861	5	6,500	7,960	12,135	—	—16,507
1862	3	800	834	1,290	—	—16,163
1863	—	—	—	—	—	—
1864	8	8,500	9,100	8,941	5,000	—12,504
1865	3	—	4,200	—	2,500	—10,804
1866	2	20,000	—	20,000	—	—10,804
1867	4	5,030	—	15,250	—	—21,024
1868	—	—	—	—	—	—
1869	—	—	—	—	—	—
1870	3	—	23,400	—	20,000	—17,624

year	no. of transactions	income (£s) mortgages	sales	expenditure (£s) purchases	redemptions	balance (£s)
1871	2	5,000	—	4,800	—	—17,424
1872	5	10,000	—	1,000	11,000	—19,424
1873	—	—	—	—	—	—
1874	4	18,000	—	1,532	—	—2,956
1875	2	—	36,798	16,761	17,500	—419
1876	5	6,000	23,830	—	9,000	+20,411
1877	—	—	—	—	—	—
1878	1	10,000	—	—	—	+30,411
1879	—	—	—	—	—	—
1880	1	725	—	—	—	+31,136
1881	—	—	—	—	—	—
1882	—	—	—	—	—	
1883	—	—	—	—	—	—
1884	1	—	1,500	—	—	+32,636
1885	2	—	600	1,400	—	+31,836
1852-85	79	120,055	111,915	134,134	66,000	

Source: P.R.O.I., incumbered estates commrs, index of conveyances, ii, 2948, 3044, 3095, 3154; iii, 3414, 3914; v, 5810, 6193; vi, 6599, 6984, 7257; Reg. Deeds, 1852/26/109-10; 1854/4/272, 15/16; 1855/8/169; 1856/6/195, 10/70; 1857/2/104, 5/51, 171-2, 14/300, 19/156, 25/91, 33/188, 36/231; 1858/1/124, 13/128, 14/16; 1859/28/267-9, 42/136, 43/155; 1860/2/172, 9/13, 11/51, 34/276; 1861/2/40, 58, 11/66, 12/232, 16/209; 1862/6/230, 10/90, 35/166; 1864/22/6, 95, 24/132, 29/30, 34/68-9, 216, 36/121; 1865/11/93, 17/152, 19/289; 1866/21/206, 36/126; 1867/1/164, 13/246, 23/130, 30/149; 1868/28/44, 30/72; 1870/10/259, 281, 31/126; 1871/1/86, 28/255; 1872/12/161, 18/211, 20/95, 25/222, 32/84; 1874/14/198, 26/84, 33/64; 1875/15/156, 283, 19/190, 20/260; 1876/1/276, 2/160, 15/269, 18/140-41, 208, 22/197-8, /85, 55/187; 1880/57/137; 1884/28/91; 1885/10/135, 18/198, 21/229.